FUNDAMENTAL PRINCIPLES OF TASAWWUF
Based on the original by Sidi Ahmad Zarruq.
AN ABRIDGEMENT BY ABD AL-RAHMAN SHA'AR.

COPYRIGHT © 2024 BY
IMAM GHAZALI PUBLISHING (USA)

ALL RIGHTS RESERVED. ASIDE FROM FAIR USE, MEANING A FEW PAGES OR LESS FOR NON-PROFIT EDUCATIONAL PURPOSES, REVIEW, OR SCHOLARLY CITATION, NO PART OF THIS PUBLICATION MAY BE REPRODUCED, STORED IN A RETRIEVAL SYSTEM, OR TRANSMITTED IN ANY FORM OR BY ANY MEANS, ELECTRONIC, MECHANICAL, PHOTOCOPYING, RECORDING, OR OTHERWISE, WITHOUT THE PRIOR PERMISSION OF THE COPYRIGHT OWNER. FOR PERMISSION REQUESTS, PLEASE WRITE TO THE PUBLISHER AT THE ADDRESS BELOW.

IMAM GHAZALI PUBLISHING
NEW YORK, USA
INFO@IMAMGHAZALI.CO
WWW.IMAMGHAZALI.CO

BULK ORDERING INFORMATION: SPECIAL DISCOUNTS ARE AVAILABLE ON QUANTITY PURCHASES. FOR DETAILS, PLEASE CONTACT THE DISTRIBUTORS:

SATTAUR PUBLISHING
INFO@SATTAURPUBLISHING.COM
WWW.SATTAURPUBLISHING.COM

PRINTED IN THE USA, UK, MALAYSIA, AND INDIA

THE VIEWS, INFORMATION, OR OPINIONS EXPRESSED ARE SOLELY THOSE OF THE AUTHOR(S) AND DO NOT NECESSARILY REPRESENT THOSE OF THE PUBLISHER.

ISBN: 978-1-966329-27-5

FIRST EDITION

10 9 8 7 6 5 4 3 2 1

Fundamental Principles of Taṣawwuf

— AN ABRIDGEMENT —

CONTENTS

The Life and Legacy of the Sheikh IX

REAL TAṢAWWUF 2

Principle 1: It is Necessary to Define *Taṣawwuf* Before Being Involved in it. 4

Principle 2: There are Many Definitions of *Taṣawwuf*. 6

Principle 3: Sincere Turning is Conditioned on it Pleasing the Real…and There is no *Taṣawwuf* without *Fiqh* (Jurisprudence). 8

Principle 4: Differing Methods do not Necessitate Different Objectives. 10

SUNNAH AND HERETICAL INNOVATION 14

Principle 5: A Thing's Prohibition due to what Occurs During it or Because of it Does Not Require the Cessation of the Foundation of its Ruling. 16

Principle 6: Patched Cloaks, the Presentation of the *Sibḥah*, the Taking of the Covenant, Shaking Hands, and Clasping Hands. 20

Principle 7: There is no Criterion except the Lawgiver. And No Appeal is to be Made Except to Him. 22

Principle 8: The False Claimants of this Path have Multiplied due to its Remoteness. 26

CONCESSIONS AND DILIGENCE 28

Principle 9: The Statements of the People of the Path Condemning Concessions and Dispensations are only Regarding Matters whose Ruling is Doubtful, not with Those Whose

Ruling is Confirmed.	30
Principle 10: The Goal is Conformity with the Truth, Even if it is in Conformity with One's Desires.	32
Principle 11: One is Rewarded in Commensurate with One's Emulation, and not Commensurate with the Difficulty One Incurs: "The Best of Your Religion is What is Easiest".	34
Principle 12: Extremism in Worship is Forbidden Just as Laxity in it is.	36

FUNDAMENTALS OF INVOCATIONS, LITANIES, AND THE GATHERINGS OF THE FOLK 38

Principle 13: The Permissibility of Practicing Invocations and Supplications Whose Meanings are Clear, even if no Authentic Narration has Mentioned Them.	40
Principle 14: Retreat is More Specific than Solitude. And in its Different Kinds and Forms, it is a Kind of I'*tikāf*.	44
Principle 15: The Lights of Invocations Burns the Traits of the Slave.	46
Principle 16: Upholding the Conditions in That for Which they are Conditions is Imperative for the Seeker.	48
Principle 17: The Invocations that are Related to Worldly Affairs Lead to Love of Allah and Attachment to His Remembrance.	50
Principle 18: The Special Quality of Each Name or Invocation is in its Meaning. Its Secret is in its Number. And the Response for it is Dependent upon the Aspiration of its Invoker.	52
Principle 19: The *Samā'* is a Dispensation with the Sufis which is Allowed Due to Need.	56
Principle 20: Whoever Listens by Way of Reality (*Ḥaqīqah*) will Obtain Realization. Whoever Listens by Way of the Ego will only Gain a Worse State.	58

FUNDAMENTALS OF ACTIONS WHILE TRAVELING THE PATH — 60

Principle 21: Knowledge is a Precondition for Action. — 62

Principle 22: Correcting One's Manner of Seeking Assists One in Attaining What He is Seeking. — 64

Principle 23: Perfection of Worship is by Upholding its External and Internal Limits without Excess or Laxity. — 66

Principle 24: The Origin of Every Good or Evil: Morsels and Association. — 68

Principle 25: Let None of You be Like the Bad Slave, Who, if he is Not Made to Fear, Does not Work. — 70

FUNDAMENTAL KNOWLEDGE FOR THE WAYFARER — 74

Principle 26: There Being Various Kinds of Good Indicates the Existence of a Variety of Approaches to Good. — 76

Principle 27: Each Science is Only Taken From Those who Dominate it. — 78

Principle 28: Whatever Emerges from the Heart Enters the Heart, while Whatever is Limited to the Tongue will not Traverse the Ears. — 80

Principle 29: Distinctions do not Necessitate Superiority. — 82

Principle 30: Speaking Surely about the Belief of a Muslim on the Sainthood of a Pious Person. — 84

Principle 31: The Tongues of Creation are the Pens of the Real. — 88

Principle 32: Precaution Regarding the Book *Talbīs Iblīs*, *al-Futūḥāt*, and Others. — 90

THE NOTIONS OF THE SOUL — 92

Principle 33: Negating Notions by Erecting Evidence of their Falsehood Causes Them to Become Entrenched in the Soul. They are Better Dispelled by Turning Away From Them. — 94

Principle 34: Distinguishing the (Source) of Notions is from the Concerns of the People of *Murāqabah* (Vigilance) in Order to Remove Distractions from the Heart.   96

THE GUIDE AND THE PLEDGE   100

Principle 35: Every Sufi that Neglects his States in his Dealing with People, According to how he has been Commanded Regarding Them, will Inevitably Fall into Error.   102

Principle 36: The Opening of Every Individual and his Light Corresponds to the Opening and Light of the One he Follows.   104

Principle 37: No One is Followed (in every Single Thing) Except the Sinless Because Error has been Prevented From Them, or Whoever's Excellence they Declare.   106

Principle 38: For the Correction of the Soul it is Necessary to Follow a Shaykh in Order to Prevent Divergence and Deviation.   110

Principle 39: Taking Knowledge and Action from the Shaykhs and Benefitting from their Aspiration and State.   114

Principle 40: The Conclusion   118

THE LIFE & LEGACY OF THE SHEIKH

Sheikh Aḥmad Zarrūq (1442–1493 CE), known as Imām al-Zarrūq al-Shādhilī, was a distinguished Moroccan scholar, jurist, and Sufi of the 15th century. He is celebrated as one of the greatest scholarly figures in Muslim history, seamlessly blending legal, theological, and spiritual sciences. Widely recognized for his contributions to the Shādhilī order, Sheikh Aḥmad Zarrūq is also regarded by many as the *mujaddid* (renewer) of his time, earning him the honorific title *"Muḥtasib al-'Ulamā' wa al-Awliyā'"* (Regulator of Scholars and Saints).

EARLY LIFE AND UPBRINGING

Sheikh Aḥmad Zarrūq was born on 7 June 1442 CE (22 Muḥarram 846 AH) in Tiliwān, a mountainous region of Morocco, and belonged to the Berber Barnūsī tribe. Orphaned within the first seven days of his life due to a devastating outbreak, he was raised by his maternal grandmother, Umm al-Banīn, a devout woman of piety and scholarship. She was instrumental in shaping his formative years, ensuring he memorized the Qur'an by the age of four and instilling in him a love for worship and the recitation of litanies. Her unique teaching methods combined discipline, spirituality, and reliance on Allah, leaving an indelible mark on her grandson.

The Imam's early education involved mastering traditional Islamic sciences, including Mālikī jurisprudence, Arabic, and hadith. By his youth, he was recognized as an authority in these disciplines, earning the respect of his contemporaries. However, his grandmother's emphasis on both outward practice and inward devotion laid the groundwork for his embrace and study of Sufism.

IN BLESSED COMPANY

Sheikh Aḥmad Zarrūq was shaped profoundly by the company of numerous scholars and righteous individuals, spanning both jurists (*fuqahā'*) and Sufis (*fuqarā'*). Their influence on his development as a scholar and spiritual master is undeniable. Among them were:

Abu al-'Abbās Aḥmad ibn Muḥammad al-Fishtālī: His maternal uncle, a devout jurist known as Nūr Allāh. He was known for completing the recitation of the entire Qur'an every three days. He performed the *taḥnīk* (ritual of sweetening an infant's palate) for the young Imam. His last words were the supplication: "Our Lord, do not let our hearts deviate after You have guided us. Grant us mercy from Yourself. Surely You are the Bestower" (*Qur'an* 3:8).

Abu Muḥammad 'Abd Allāh ibn Muḥammad ibn Mūsā al-'Abdusī: A righteous spiritual guide and jurist who served as the Mufti of Fez. He eradicated numerous innovations in Morocco, upheld justice, and ensured the enforcement of rights. A man of great simplicity, he passed away leaving only a few garments, two sets of *iḥrām* clothing, and the *Shamā'il* of al-Tirmidhī, which he never let out of his hands.

Abu al-'Abbās Aḥmad Ibn al-'Ijl al-Wazārwālī: The judge of al-Madīnat al-Bayḍā' and deputy of the judge of Old Fez. He completed the recitation of the Qur'an weekly.

Sheikh Abu al-'Abbās Aḥmad ibn Sa'īd al-Miknāsī: A preacher at the Qarawiyyīn Mosque, renowned for his eloquence and dedication.

Abu al-Ḥasan 'Alī ibn 'Abd al-Raḥmān al-Anfāsī: The preacher and imam of the al-Andalus Mosque, remembered for leading prayers for rain.

Abu ʿAbd Allāh Muḥammad, known as Ibn Amlāl: A Sheikh and prominent jurist who was a distinguished scholar and Mufti for the Muslim community.

Abu ʿAlī al-Ḥasan Ibn Mandīl al-Maghīlī: A learned Sheikh, jurist, judge, teacher, ḥadīth expert (ḥāfiẓ), and imam at the Ināniyyah Madrasa.

Abu ʿAbd Allāh Muḥammad, known as al-ʿAṭṭār: A devout seeker who spent 21 days at the maqām of Sheikh Abu Yaʿazzā, where he dreamed of the Sheikh directly imparting knowledge to him.

Abu al-ʿAbbās ibn ʿAlī ibn Ṣāliḥ, known as al-Filālī: A virtuous jurist and Sufi who often remarked, "To have a good opinion of Allah is more fitting than a bad opinion of Him."

Sidi Abu Zakariyyā: The leader of al-Zahrā, a virtuous Sheikh revered for his humility. Known for dressing modestly to avoid undue attention, he was deeply loved and respected by his community.

HIS SCHOLARLY JOURNEY AND SPIRITUAL DEVELOPMENT

Sheikh Aḥmad Zarrūq began his formal studies in Fez, enrolling at the prestigious Qarawiyyīn and ʿInāniyyah. He studied under more than thirty-five scholars, including prominent figures such as Imām ʿAbd al-Raḥmān Ath-Thaʿlabī and Imām Muḥammad ibn ʿAlī al-Bistī al-Qalsādī. He excelled in Mālikī fiqh, uṣūl (principles of Islamic jurisprudence), and grammar, becoming a teacher and jurist at a young age.

Despite his grounding in the outward sciences, Sheikh Aḥmad's heart yearned for spiritual fulfillment. His turning point came when he met Sheikh ʿAbdullāh al-Makkī, under whom he undertook his formal initiation into the Shādhilī path. This relationship was transformative but not without challenges. On one occasion, the Imam misjudged his teacher upon witnessing an ambiguous spiritual vision. Sheikh al-Makkī rebuked him, leading to a period of deep reflection and repentance. Sheikh Aḥmad Zarrūq eventually reconciled with his teacher, continuing his spiritual journey with renewed humility.

After leaving Fez, Sheikh Aḥmad Zarrūq traveled extensively. He performed the Hajj and studied in Makkah, Madinah, and Egypt. In Cairo, he became a disciple of Sheikh Abu'l-'Abbās al-Ḥaḍramī, who became his primary spiritual guide. The Imam's time in Cairo marked a period of significant spiritual illumination, as he attained mastery in devotional practices (*awrad*) and was acknowledged with permission as a spiritual guide in his own right.

ON HIS HAJJ

Sheikh Aḥmad Zarrūq embarked on his first pilgrimage (Ḥajj) with remarkable faith and resolve despite having no tangible financial means. When he decided to undertake the journey and made firm intention on the idea, he did not possess even a single silver dirham. On the day of his departure from his hometown, his only asset was a donkey. During this journey, he stopped in Cairo to study under Imam Muḥammad al-Sakhāwī, a leading murīd of Ibn Ḥajar al-'Asqalānī.

On his second pilgrimage, the Imam set out once again with nothing more than a donkey and a few books, which were of no assistance in covering his expenses. Nonetheless, his dedication to the Hajj remained unwavering. Over the course of his life, Sheikh Aḥmad Zarrūq performed the Hajj seven times, each under similar circumstances.

TEACHING AND INFLUENCE

Sheikh Aḥmad Zarrūq's scholarly reputation attracted widespread attention. At Al-Azhar in Cairo, he held a teaching post as the lead Mālikī jurist, lecturing to audiences of nearly six thousand attendees. A specially constructed chair symbolized his authority and remains a testament to his enduring influence. His lessons were attended by students and scholars from all walks of life, including both the elite and the common people. His ability to harmonize the exoteric and esoteric dimensions of Islam made him a beacon of guidance for seekers of knowledge and spirituality alike.

Later, Sheikh Aḥmad relocated to Libya, settling in Misrata. There, he established a thriving spiritual and educational center, revitalizing the Shādhilī order. His leadership attracted committed disciples and solidified the Zarrūqiyyah branch of the Shādhilī path. His spiritual state inspired awe and devotion, with countless accounts of his divine favor and standing with Allah being passed down. One such incident involved a band of highway robbers repenting after witnessing Sheikh Aḥmad Zarrūq's spiritual standing, with their descendants continuing to serve the Zarrūqiyyah *zāwiyah* to this day.

LITERARY CONTRIBUTIONS

Sheikh Aḥmad Zarrūq authored over fifty works spanning jurisprudence, theology, and Sufism. Among his most notable writings are:

- *Qawāʿid al-Taṣawwuf* (*The Principles of Sufism*), a foundational text synthesizing Sufi ethics and practice with Islamic law. The work at hand is an abridgement of the original.
- Commentaries on Ibn ʿAṭā Allāh's *Ḥikam*, including

thirty unique expositions of this seminal Sufi work.
* A commentary on *Dalā'il al-Khayrāt* by Imām al-Jazūlī.
* Treatises such as *Al-Nasā'iḥ al-Kāfiyah* and *Al-'Aqā'id al-Khams*, which address practical and theological aspects of Sufism.

Sheikh Aḥmad Zarrūq also composed poetry and personal reflections, leaving behind an autobiographical journal documenting his daily experiences, insights, and growth.

LEGACY AND PASSING

Sheikh Aḥmad Zarrūq passed away in 899 AH (1493 CE) in Misrata, Libya, at the age of 63. His *maqām*, housed within a mosque and shrine, became a revered site for Muslim visitors. Despite its desecration by militants in recent years, his spiritual legacy endures through the works he authored and the legacy he inspired. His synthesis of outward and inward spirituality continues to influence Islamic thought.

Fundamental Principles of Taṣawwuf

— AN ABRIDGEMENT —

مختصر قواعد التصوف

REAL TAṢAWWUF

حقيقة التصوف

PRINCIPLE I: IT IS NECESSARY TO DEFINE TAṢAWWUF BEFORE BEING INVOLVED IN IT.

The discussion of any topic or thing stems from the conceptualization of its essence, its benefit, and its substance through a self-evident or acquired intellectual understanding. The objective is to apply the appropriate measure – namely of rejection or acceptance – to each matter, thereby establishing its origin and its details.

Consequently, it necessarily precedes one's investigation of it, as a form of clearly identifying it, encouraging others in it and allusion to its contents. Thus, you must understand well!

قاعدة ١ ضرورة تعريف التصوف قبل الخوض فيه

الكلامُ في الشيء فرعُ تصوُّرِ ماهيَّتِه وفائدتِه ومادَّتِه، بشعورٍ ذهني مُكتسَبٍ أو بديهيٍّ، ليرجعَ إليه في أفراد ما وقع عليه ردًّا وقبولًا، وتأصيلًا وتفصيلًا.

فلزم تقديمُ ذلك على الخوض فيه، إعلامًا به وتحضيضًا عليه، وإيماءًا لمعادنه، فافهم.

PRINCIPLE 2: THERE ARE MANY DEFINITIONS OF TAṢAWWUF.

The essence of something is its reality. Its reality is that to which it points and reflects in its entirety. Knowledge of that can be gained either through a definition, a description, or an explanation. The first is more encompassing, the second is more illustrative and clearer, and the last is more complete in terms of its clarity and being swiftly understood.

Taṣawwuf has been defined, described, and explained in nearly 2,000 manners. All of them point to and endorse the sincere turning toward Allah ﷻ. The rest are only aspects of that. And Allah knows best.

قاعدة ٢ تعدد تعريفات التصوف

ماهية الشيء: حقيقته، وحقيقته: ما دَلَّت عليه جملتُه. وتعريف ذلك بحد: وهو أجمع، أو رسمٍ: وهو أوضح، أو تفسيرٍ: وهو أتمُّ لبيانه وسرعةِ فهمِه.

وقد حُدّ التصوف ورُسِمَ وفُسِّرَ بوجوه تبلغ نحو الألفين، ترجعُ كلُّها لصدق التوجه إلى الله تعالى، وإنّما هي وجوه فيه، والله أعلم.

PRINCIPLE 3: SINCERE TURNING IS CONDITIONED ON IT PLEASING THE REAL... AND THERE IS NO TAṢAWWUF WITHOUT FIQH (JURISPRUDENCE).

Sincere turning is conditioned on it being performed for the satisfaction of the Real ﷻ and through means that satisfy Him. Additionally, a conditioned thing is not possible without its requisite conditions being fulfilled, for He is not satisfied with disbelief from His servants.[1] It is thus necessary to study ʿaqīdah (creed). "And if you are grateful, He will be satisfied with that for you."[2] Accordingly, it is imperative to act upon Islam and its dictates. As such, there is no *taṣawwuf* without *fiqh*, because Allah's regulations regarding outward practice can only be known through it. Nor is there any *fiqh* without *taṣawwuf* because no act counts without there being sincere turning to Him. Nor is any one of them valid without faith, because neither of them is valid without it.

Therefore, it is imperative to combine all three elements in light of their rulings being dependent upon one another. It is like the interdependence of the spirits and the bodies, for the former units cannot exist except inside of them. And bodies can have no life without them.

Of this import is the statement of Mālik ﷺ, "Whoever practices *taṣawwuf* without jurisprudence commits heresy. Whoever learns jurisprudence but does not practice *taṣawwuf* contravenes. And whoever joins between them will have both of them realized."

I say, "The first disbelieves because he will (inevitably) claim co-action, which leads to negating the Divine wisdom and

---

(1) *al-Zumar*, 7.
(2) *al-Zumar*, 7.

قاعدة ٣ صدق التوجه مشروط برضا الحق.. ولا تصوف إلا بفقه.

صِدقُ التوجُّهِ مشروطٌ بكونه مِنْ حيث يرضاه الحق تعالى وبما يرضاه، ولا يصح مشروط بدون شرطه؛ ﴿وَلَا يَرۡضَىٰ لِعِبَادِهِ ٱلۡكُفۡرَۖ﴾، فلزم تحقيق الإيمان؛ ﴿وَإِن تَشۡكُرُواْ يَرۡضَهُ لَكُمۡۗ﴾ فلزم العمل بالإسلام.

فلا تصوف إلا بفقه؛ إذ لا تُعرف أحكام الله الظاهرة إلا منه، ولا فقه إلا بتصوف، إذ لا عمل إلا بصدق توجه، ولا هما إلا بإيمان، إذ لا يصح واحد منهما بدونه، فلزم الجميع لتلازمها في الحكم، كتلازم الأرواح للأجساد، إذ لا وجود لها إلا فيها، كما لا حياة لها إلا بها، فافهم.

ومنه قول مالك رحمه الله: (من تصوف ولم يتفقه فقد تزندق، ومن تفقه ولم يتصوف فقد تفسق، ومن جمع بينهما فقد تحقق).

قلت: تَزَنۡدَقَ الأول: لأنَّه قائلٌ بالجبر الموجب لنفي الحكمة والأحكام.

وتَفَسَّقَ الثاني: لخلو عمله عن صدق التوجه الحاجز عن معصية الله تعالى، وعن الإخلاص المُشترطِ في العمل لله.

decrees. The second has transgressed due to his actions lacking any sincere orientation, which prevents one from disobeying Allah ﷻ; as such, it lacks the very sincerity upon which acting for Allah depends. The third has become realized because he has upheld the overarching reality through the lens of adhering to the truth. Know this and understand well.

وتحقَّقَ الثالث: لقيامه بالحقيقة في عين التمسك بالحق، فاعرف ذلك وافهم.

PRINCIPLE 4: DIFFERING METHODS DO NOT NECESSITATE DIFFERENT OBJECTIVES.

Differing methods do not logically require dissimilar objectives. Rather, the objective may be one despite there being divergent methods. For example, worship, asceticism, and knowledge are all different methods for attaining the proximity of the Real through His grace. Yet, they are all interconnected.

Therefore, the gnostic must worship. Otherwise, his knowledge is of no consequence, since he fails to worship the One he knows. Likewise, he must exercise the teachings of asceticism. Otherwise, he has no reality because he did not turn away from everyone apart from Him.

Likewise, they (gnosis and asceticism) are imperative for worshippers because there can be no worship without knowledge. Neither can one be free for worship except through asceticism.

The same applies to asceticism, as it cannot exist in its true form except with gnosis. Nor can there be any true asceticism without worship. Otherwise, it becomes aimless.

Certainly, whoever is preoccupied with action is a worshipper. Whoever is preoccupied with abstinence is an ascetic, and whoever is preoccupied with observing the work of the Real is a gnostic. Yet, in any case they are all Sufis. And Allah knows best.

قاعدة ٤ اختلاف المسالك لا يلزم منه اختلاف المقصد

لا يلزم من اختلاف المسالك اختلاف المقصد، بل قد يكون متحدا مع اختلاف مسالكه، كالعبادة والزهادة والمعرفة مسالكُ لقرب الحق على سبيل الكرامة، وكلها متداخلة، فلا بد للعارف من عبادة، وإلا فلا عبرة بمعرفته إذا لم يعبد معروفه.

ولا بد له من زهادة، وإلا فلا حقيقة عنده، إذ لم يُعرض عمن سواه.

ولا بد للعابد منهما؛ إذ لا عبادة إلا بمعرفة، ولا فراغ للعبادة إلا بزهد.

والزاهد كذلك إذ لا زهد إلا بمعرفة، ولا زهد إلا بعبادة، وإلا عاد بطالة.

نعم مَنْ غلبَ عليه العملُ فعابد، أو التركُ فزاهد، أو النظرُ لتصريف الحق فعارف، والكلّ صوفية، والله أعلم.

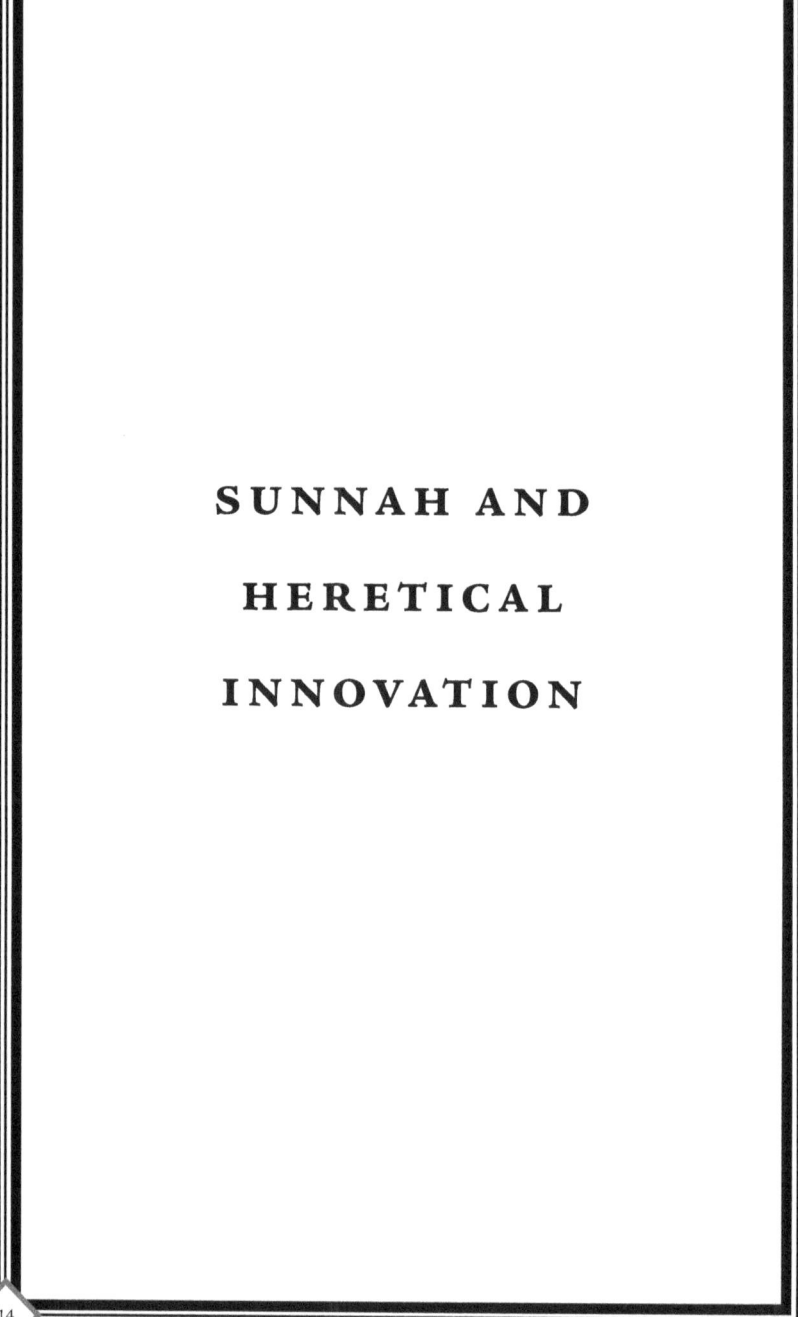

SUNNAH AND HERETICAL INNOVATION

السنة والبدعة

PRINCIPLE 5: A THING'S PROHIBITION DUE TO WHAT OCCURS DURING IT OR BECAUSE OF IT DOES NOT REQUIRE THE CESSATION OF ITS FOUNDATIONAL RULING.

The prohibition of something on account of what occurs during it or because of it does not necessarily indicate the cessation of its foundational ruling.

The later Sufi researchers had insisted, along with the majority of the jurists, on the prohibition of *samāʿ*[3] because of the firm grip that heretical innovations had taken at the time, and because of the misguidance that has been caused by it. In fact, al-Ḥātimī ﷺ said, "*Samāʿ* in this age cannot be encouraged by any Muslim. Nor can any shaykh be followed who practices or encourages *samāʿ*.

Shaykh Abū al-Ḥasan al-Shādhilī ﷺ said, "I asked my teacher about *samāʿ*. He said to me, 'Indeed, they found their fathers in waywardness. Thus, they hastened to follow their footsteps.'"[4]

Ibn Nujayd ﷺ said, "A slip in *samāʿ* is worse than falling into such and such a thing. It is a practice that has maligned some people."

It was said to al-Junayd, "You used to attend and listen (to the *samāʿ*). Why did you leave it?" He replied, "From whom[5]?" The asker said, "From Allah." So, he (al-Junayd) replied, "And who am I with?"

Its ruling of prohibition is along the same lines as that of gathering for divine remembrance. It is further emphasized

---

(3) A Sufi practice that involved gathering to listen to sung words of spiritual or religious poetry. It may involve musical instruments, ecstatic movements, or other practices.
(4) al-Ṣāffāt, 69-70.
(5) i.e. "To whom was I listening?"

قاعدة ٥ منع الشيء لما يعرض فيه أو بسببه، لا يقضي بنقض أصل حكمه

منعُ الشيء لما يعرض فيه أو بسببه، لا يقضي بنقض أصلِ حكمه، وقد جزم محققو المتأخرين من الصوفية وأكثر الفقهاء بمنع السماع لعارض الوقت من الابتداع والضلال بسببه، حتى قال الحاتمي رحمه الله:

(السماع في هذا الزمان لا يقول به مسلم، ولا يقتدى بشيخ يعمل بالسماع أو يقول به).

وقال الشيخ أبو الحسن الشاذلي رضي الله عنه:

(سألت أستاذي عن السماع فقال لي: ﴿إِنَّهُمْ أَلْفَوْا۟ ءَابَآءَهُمْ ضَآلِّينَ ۝ فَهُمْ عَلَىٰٓ ءَاثَٰرِهِمْ يُهْرَعُونَ ۝﴾.

وقال ابن نجيد رحمه الله: (زلة في السماع، شر من كذا وكذا سنة تغتاب الناس).

وقيل للجنيد: كنت تسمع، فلم تَركت؟

قال: (ممن)؟ قيل له: مِنَ الله. قال: فَمَعَ مَنْ أنا؟ انتهى.

ومجرى الحكم في المنع كالذكر بالجمع، يأكد لنقد حكم الأصل،

when the foundation of its (original) ruling is not found. Thus, those who prefer rulings meant to cut off the avenues to evil prohibit it completely, while others only prohibit whatever falsehood may occur in it, and nothing beyond that. And Allah ﷻ knows best.

فالقائل بسد الذرائع يمنع بالجملة، وغيره يمنع ما تَصَوَّرَ فيه الباطلُ ليس إلّا. والله سبحانه أعلم.

PRINCIPLE 6: PATCHED CLOAKS, THE PRESENTATION OF THE SIBḤAH, THE TAKING OF THE COVENANT, SHAKING HANDS, AND CLASPING HANDS.

Wearing patched clothing, the presentation of the *sibḥah*, taking the covenant, shaking hands, and clasping hands are from the knowledge of transmission. This is unless a certain state is sought through them, in which case they are for that state's sake.

Ibn Abī Jamrah cited the taking of the covenant in the chapter on the prophetic pact (*bayʿah*), and deemed it to be one of its categories. And the people of the path took wearing patched clothing from the Hadiths that have been narrated regarding him ﷺ cutting patches from his own cloak for more than one of his Companions. Likewise, the taking of the pledge of Salamah ibn al-Akwaʿ is evidence of it (the pledge) containing a secret. Similarly, his ﷺ taking the pledge of his Companions after their faith had been established and firmly instilled in their hearts was solely for that reason. And the ruling regarding inheritance and emulation is present in it just as in every other inherited practice. Additionally, it cannot be downright disavowed due to the existence of a difference of opinion over it. Nor is it obligatory because there is uncertainty regarding it.

This is not the place to discuss its manner and methodology, yet it is for the lover, the adherent, or the realized person. It contains hidden secrets that are known by its people. And Allah knows best.

قاعدة ٦ الخِرقة، ومناولة السبحة، وأخذ العهد والمصافحة والمشابكة

إلباس الخِرقة، ومناولة السبحة، وأخذ العهد، والمصافحةُ والمشابكةُ مِنْ علم الرواية، إلا أن يقصد بها حال فتكون لأجله.

وقد ذكر ابن أبي جمرة أخذَ العهد في باب البيعة وألحقه بأقسامها، وأخذوا إلباس الخِرقة من أحاديث وردت في خلعه ﷺ على غير واحد من أصحابه، ومبايعةُ سلمة بن الأكوع تشهد لإيداع السر فيها، وكذا مبايعته ﷺ لأصحابه بعد تحقق الإيمان وتقرُّرِه في قلوبهم إنما هو لذلك، ويجري حكم الإرث والتأسي فيها كغيرها، فلا نكير؛ لجري الخلاف، ولا لزوم؛ لوجود الاشتباه.

ووجهُها وطريقُها ليس هذا محله. نعم، هي لمحب أو منتسب أو محقق، وفيها أسرار خفية يعلمها أهلها، والله أعلم.

PRINCIPLE 7: THERE IS NO CRITERION EXCEPT THE LAWGIVER, AND NO APPEAL IS TO BE MADE EXCEPT TO HIM.

There is no yardstick except the Lawgiver, so no appeal can be made except to Him. Allah ﷻ said: "O, you who believe, obey Allah and obey the Messenger and those charged with authority among you. If you dispute about anything, refer it to Allah and His Messenger if you are indeed believers in Allah and the Last Day. That is better and a more excellent interpretation."[6]

And He had obligated some things, prohibited others, recommended some, disliked others, and permitted another category. And the scholars clarified that which had come from Him, each of them by way of His own evidence. Thus, it is necessary to refer to their principles in such matters without contravening the truth or abandoning true speech.

It follows then that whoever transgresses against the first two categories (obligations and prohibitions), he is rejected in what is agreed upon. And where there is disagreement, the ruling of the Imam that he follows is enacted upon him; he is not rebuked except for that which is agreed upon in his *madhhab*, that is, if he repeatedly does the act without a legal necessity. Otherwise, the topic of legal necessity has its own rulings.

With regard to that which falls beyond the obligatory or the prohibited matters, no one has any right to rebuke another. If his ruling is confirmed from the viewpoint of his school, is not connected to the rights of others, and the matter does not cause him to reach the level of neglect or his situation does not indicate his disregard for the religion or taking it lightly, then he is to be left alone. "Many a person who eats and is grateful is

---

(6)   *al-Nisā'*, 59.

قاعدة ٧ لا حاكم إلا الشارع ولا تحاكم إلا له.

لا حاكمَ إلا الشارعُ، فلا تحاكمَ إلا له، قال الله تعالى:

﴿يَٰٓأَيُّهَا ٱلَّذِينَ ءَامَنُوٓاْ أَطِيعُواْ ٱللَّهَ وَأَطِيعُواْ ٱلرَّسُولَ وَأُوْلِي ٱلۡأَمۡرِ مِنكُمۡۖ فَإِن تَنَٰزَعۡتُمۡ فِي شَيۡءٖ فَرُدُّوهُ إِلَى ٱللَّهِ وَٱلرَّسُولِ إِن كُنتُمۡ تُؤۡمِنُونَ بِٱللَّهِ وَٱلۡيَوۡمِ ٱلۡأٓخِرِۚ ذَٰلِكَ خَيۡرٞ وَأَحۡسَنُ تَأۡوِيلًا ٥٩﴾.

وقد أوجب وحرم وندب، وكره وأباح، وبين العلماء ما جاء عنه، كلٌّ بوجهه ودليله، فلزم الرجوع لأصولهم في ذلك من غير تعدٍّ للحق، ولا خروجٍ عن الصدق.

فمن أخل بالأولين، اطُّرِحَ حيث يُتَّفَقُ إجماعا، وحيث يُخْتَلَفُ اعتُبِرَ إمامُهُ في حكمه، فلا يُنكَّرُ عليه غيرُ مَا اتُّفِقَ عليه بمذهبه، إن تكرر لغير ضرورة، وإلا فالضرورة لها أحكام.

وما بعد الواجب والمحرم ليس لأحد على أحد فيه سبيل، إن أثبتَ حكمه على وجهه، ولم يتعلق بغيرِ تركه، ولم يخرج به الأمرُ لحدِّ التهاون، أو تشهد أحوالُه بالإزراء على ذلك ورِقَّةِ الدِّيانة به، (فَرُبَّ طاعمٍ شاكرٍ، خيرٌ مِنْ صائمٍ صابر) الحديث.

ومِنْ ثَمَّ أجمعَ القوم على أنهم لا يوقظون نائما، ولا يُصوِّمون مُفْطِرًا

better than the patient faster", as the Hadith states.

It is along from this vantage point that the people of the path have agreed that they would not wake a sleeping person, nor force someone averse to fasting to fast, from the perspective that pride and showing off may affect his work. Additionally, this is the case since helping one another to uphold religious obligations is the basis and not anything else. The entirety of the Sunnah testifies to that. And Allah ﷻ knows best.

مِنْ وجهِ دخول الرياء والتكلف، ولأن العناية بإقامة الفرائض هي الأصل لا غيرها، وكلُّ السُّنّةِ تشهدُ لذلك، والله سبحانه أعلم.

PRINCIPLE 8: THE FALSE CLAIMANTS OF THIS PATH HAVE MULTIPLIED DUE TO ITS REMOTENESS.

The false claimants have multiplied in this path due to its remoteness. And its understanding has become rare due to its subtlety. Criticism of its people has increased due to its purity. And the sincere advisers have warned against trekking it due to the frequent errors that occur in it.

The Imams wrote books refuting its people due to what the people of misguidance have innovated and introduced in it, and what they have attributed to it. It reached the point that Ibn al-ʿArabī al-Ḥātimī ﷺ said, "Beware of this path, because most of the Khawārij emerged from it. And what is it but a path of either destruction or triumph? Whoever becomes gathered in its knowledge, its acts, and its states attains eternal nobility. And whoever abandons realization perishes and his pursuit is futile."

For that reason, some of the people of the path alluded to his (Ibn al-ʿArabī's) statement, "We reached a limit at which, if one stumbles just a little, he will stumble into the Fire."

We ask Allah for wellbeing through His grace and generosity.

قاعدة ٨ كثر المدعون في هذا الطريق لغربته

كثُرَ المدَّعون في هذا الطريق لغربته، وبَعُدَت الأفهامُ عنه لدقَّته، وكثُرَ الإنكارُ على أهله لنظافته، وحذَّرَ الناصحون مِنْ سلوكه لكثرة الغلط فيه.

وصنف الأئمة في الرد على أهله لما أَحْدَثَ أهلُ الضلال فيه، وما انتسبوا منه إليه، حتى قال ابن العربي الحاتمي رحمه الله: (احذر هذا الطريق، فإنَّ أكثرَ الخوارج إنما خرجوا منه، وما هو إلا طريقُ الهُلك أو المُلك، مَنْ حقَّقَ علمه وعمله وحاله، نال عزَّ الأبد، ومَنْ فارقَ التحقيق فيه، هَلَكَ وما نَفَذَ، ولذلك أشار بعضهم بقوله: بلغنا إلى حدٍّ إذ مالَ هكذا، مال في النار، نسأل الله العافية بمنه وكرمه).

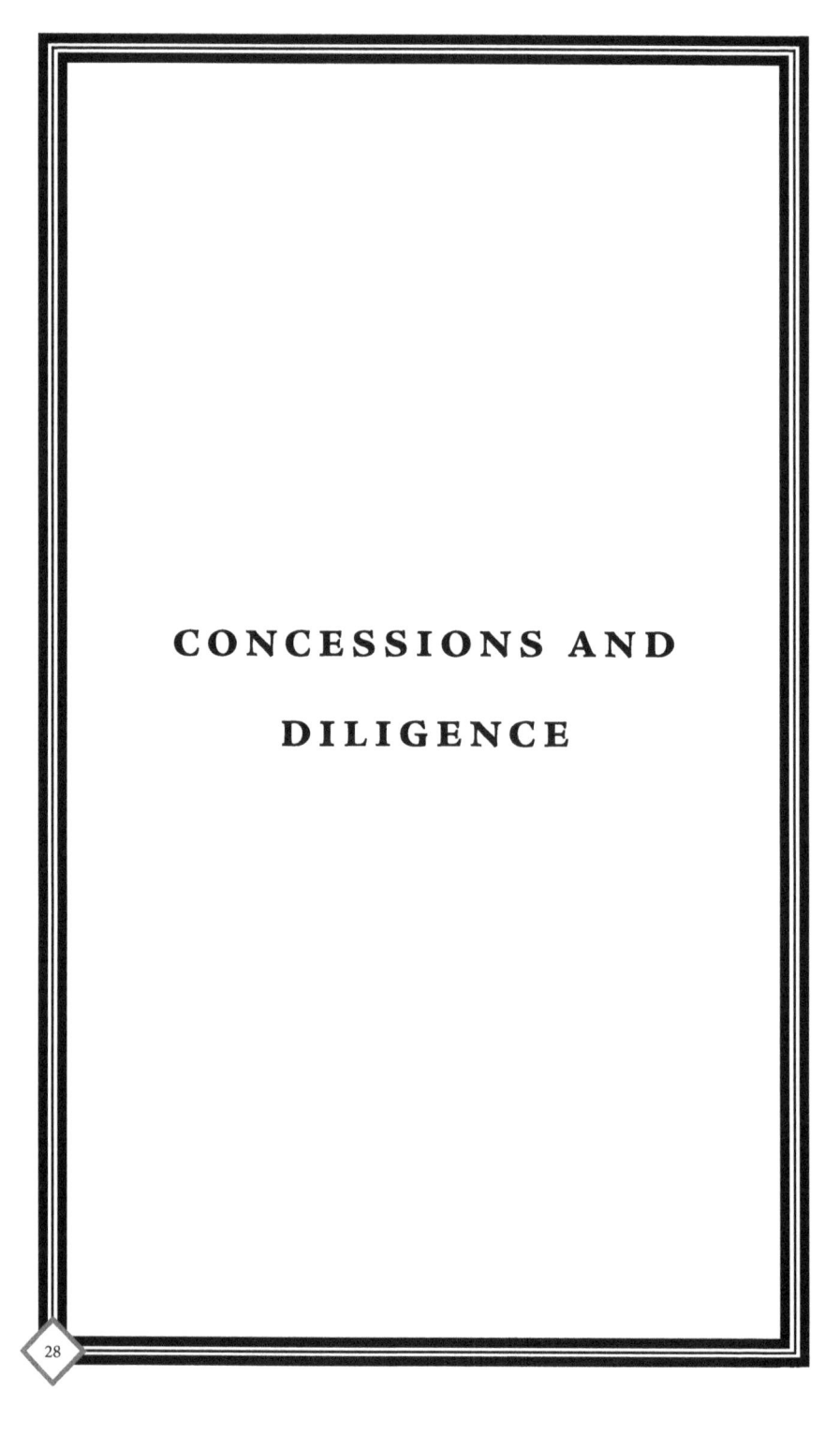

CONCESSIONS AND DILIGENCE

الرخصة والعزيمة

PRINCIPLE 9: THE STATEMENTS OF THE PEOPLE OF THE PATH CONDEMNING CONCESSIONS AND DISPENSATIONS ARE ONLY REGARDING MATTERS WHOSE RULING IS DOUBTFUL, NOT WITH THOSE WHOSE RULING IS CONFIRMED.

Worship is to fulfil what has been ordered legislatively with respect to habitual or non-habitual actions. It is the same whether what is ordered comprises a concession or a diligence, because the command of Allah in both is the same. Therefore, ablution is not better than *tayammum* when the latter is permissible. Nor is fasting better than eating when the latter is necessary. Likewise, performing a complete prayer is not better than shortening it when the latter has been ordered.

It is about this very matter that he ﷺ made the statement, "Indeed, Allah loves that a concession is taken just as He hates for diligence to be abandoned when He has commanded it." This statement is not regarding concessions whose rulings are differed upon because caution has been prescribed vis-à-vis everything whose ruling is doubtful, unlike when they have been confirmed, for leaving this latter type is excess. And it is regarding the former type that the people of the path made their statements condemning concessions and dispensations.

And Allah knows best.

قاعدة 9 محمل كلام القوم في ذم الرخص والتأويلات هو في كل مشكوك الحكم لا في المحقق.

العبادة: إقامة ما طلب شرعا من الأعمال الخارجة عن العادة، أو الداخلة، سواء كان رخصة أو عزيمة، إذ أمر الله فيهما واحد، فليس الوضوء بأولى من التيمم في محله، ولا الصوم بأولى من الإفطار في محله، ولا الإكمال بأولى من القصر في موضعه.

وعليه يتنزل قوله ﷺ: (إن الله يحب أن تؤتى رخصه كما يكره أن تترك عزائمه). لا على الرخصة المختلف في حكمها، إذ الورع مطلوب في كل مشكوك الحكم، بخلاف المحقق، فإنَّ تركه تنطُّعٌ، وعلى هذا الأخير يتنزل كلام القوم في ذم الرخص والتأويلات، والله أعلم.

PRINCIPLE 10: THE GOAL IS CONFORMITY WITH THE TRUTH, EVEN IF IT IS IN CONFORMITY WITH ONE'S DESIRES.

The goal is conformity with the truth, even if it corresponds to one's desires. Along these lines is the statement of ʿUmar ibn ʿAbd al-ʿAzīz ﷺ, "If the truth corresponds to one's desire, then it's like honey mixed with butter."

Some people engrossed themselves in contradicting (the desires of) their soul until they contradicted the truth in the midst of that endeavour. From that is their taking leave in that which is obligatory and necessary, which cannot possibly be left. And they also left a number of Sunnahs due to their popularity, even going as far as leaving those to which they had become accustomed.

Even if this has an effect on the soul, it is an avenue to falsehood and pushes its practitioner in the opposite direction of the intended moral objective. We ask Allah for freedom from that.

قاعدة ١٠ المقصود موافقة الحق حتى إن كان موافقا للهوى

المقصود موافقة الحق وإنْ كان موافقا للهوى، حتى قال عمر بن عبد العزيز ﵁: (إذا وافق الحق الهوى، فذلك الشَّهْدُ بالزبد).

وقد أغرق قوم في مخالفة النفس، حتى خالفوا الحقَّ في طي ذلك، ومنه استئذانهم في الواجب والضروري الذي لا يمكن انفكاكه، وتركهم جملة من السنن، لإلفها مع ترك ما أُلِفَ منها.

وهذا وإن كان مؤثرا في النفس، فهو مثير للباطل وصايرٌ بصاحبه لعكس القصد، نسأل الله العافية.

PRINCIPLE 11: ONE IS REWARDED IN COMMENSURATE WITH ONE'S EMULATION, AND NOT COMMENSURATE WITH THE DIFFICULTY ONE INCURS: "THE BEST OF YOUR RELIGION IS WHAT IS EASIEST."

Rewards are proportionate to one's emulation and not according to the difficulty that they incur. This is owing to the superiority of faith, knowledge, remembrance, and recitation over many other bodily movements which are more difficult than them.

His ﷺ statement, "Your reward is according to your difficulty" is regarding the elect in a specific set of circumstances. It does not imply that it is a universal rule, especially when he was not given the choice between two matters except that he chose the easiest of them. And he ﷺ also said, "The most knowledgeable of you and the most God-fearing is me." And it has also been related that, "The best of your religion is that which is easiest" as well as other reports.

And Allah knows best.

قاعدة ١١ الأجر على قدر الاتباع لا على قدر المشقة و (خير دينكم أَيْسَرُهُ)

الأجر على قدر الاتباع، لا على قدر المشقة؛ لفضل الإيمان والمعرفة والذكر والتلاوة على ما هو أشق منها بكثير من الحركات الجسمانية.

وقوله ﷺ: (أَجْرُكِ عَلَى قَدْرِ نَصَبِكِ) إخبارٌ خاصٌّ في خاصٍّ لا يلزم عمومه.

سيما وما خُيِّرَ في أمرين إلا اختار أيسرهما، مع قوله: (إن أعلمكم بالله وأتقاكم لله أنا)، وكذا جاء: (خَيْرُ دِينِكُمْ أَيْسَرُهُ) إلى غير ذلك، والله أعلم.

PRINCIPLE 12: EXTREMISM IN WORSHIP IS FORBIDDEN JUST AS LAXITY IN IT IS.

Extremism in worship is forbidden, just like how laxity in it is prohibited. Moderation, which is to take from both sides, is the most excellent of affairs, as it has been narrated (in a report), "The best of matters are the most moderate of them."

"And those who, when they spend, are not wasteful nor miserly. Rather, they stand between those."[7]

"And do not recite too loudly in your prayer, nor be silent in it. Rather, follow a path between them."[8]

He ﷺ also said, "As for me, I stand in prayer and I sleep. I fast and I leave fasting."

And he ﷺ used to stand half of the night and a third to two-thirds of it. That is the middle ground when compared to the one who stands all of it or only a small part of it.

Likewise, he ﷺ diverted Ibn ʿUmar to the middle ground by fasting half of the time, standing half of the night, completing the Qur'an in seven days, and other things.

Thus, moderation is imperative in every matter of exertion because it is easier on the soul and makes one's endurance in worship easier.

---

(7) al-Furqān, 67.
(8) al-Isrā', 110.

قاعدة ١٢ التشديد في العبادة منهي عنه، كالتراخي عنها

التشديد في العبادة منهي عنه، كالتراخي عنها. والتوسط: أخذ بالطرفين، فهو أحسن الأمور كما جاء: (خير الأمور أوساطها).

﴿وَٱلَّذِينَ إِذَآ أَنفَقُواْ لَمۡ يُسۡرِفُواْ وَلَمۡ يَقۡتُرُواْ وَكَانَ بَيۡنَ ذَٰلِكَ قَوَامٗا ۝٦٧﴾، ﴿وَلَا تَجۡهَرۡ بِصَلَاتِكَ وَلَا تُخَافِتۡ بِهَا وَٱبۡتَغِ بَيۡنَ ذَٰلِكَ سَبِيلٗا ۝١١٠﴾.

وقال ﷺ: (أما أنا فأقوم وأنام، وأصوم وأفطر) الحديث.

وكان يقوم من الليل نصفه، وثلثه إلى ثلثيه، وهو الوسط باعتبار من يأتي على كله، أو لا يقوم منه إلا اليسير.

وكذلك رد عبد الله بن عمر للوسط بصيام نصف الدهر وقيام نصف الليل، وختم القرآن في سبع إلى غير ذلك، فلزم التوسط في كل مكتسب، لأنه أرفق بالنفوس وأبقى للعبادة.

FUNDAMENTALS OF INVOCATIONS, LITANIES, AND THE GATHERINGS OF THE FOLK

ضوابط الذكر والأوراد ومجالس القوم

PRINCIPLE 13: THE PERMISSIBILITY OF PRACTICING INVOCATIONS AND SUPPLICATIONS WHOSE MEANINGS ARE CLEAR, EVEN IF NO AUTHENTIC NARRATION HAS MENTIONED THEM.

The domain of legislation has declared as permissible the practice of invocations and supplications whose meanings are well-defined, even if no authentic narration has mentioned them. This was indicated by Ibn al-ʿArabī, al-Sirāj, and other scholars.

Furthermore, there have come Hadiths on the benefit of supplications upon the tongue of the slave that emerge from his own ambition. In fact, Mālik ☙ included in his *Muwaṭṭa'*, in the chapter on his ☙ supplication, the statement of Abū al-Dardāʾ, "The eyes have slept, the eyelids have become heavy, and all that remains is You, O Living, O Self-sustaining."

The Prophet ☙ said to the one who supplicated with the words, "I ask You by the fact that You are Allah. There is no god but You, the One, the Absolute ...", "You have supplicated Allah by His Greatest Name".

He responded in a similar manner to the one who supplicated with the words, "O Most Loving! O Most Loving! O Lord of the Majestic Throne."

These are a myriad of proofs that everything whose meaning is clear is good in and of itself. As such, it is good to act upon it, whether supported by a legislative source or not. Examples include a good dream or the inspiration of someone whose distinction has been verified, such as the supplications of al-Shādhilī, al-Nawawī, or others.

However, in the supplication of Ibn Sabʿīn, there are many ambiguous and spurious utterances. As such, it is imperative to avoid them completely, due to the danger that they contain. The only exception in this regard is a scholar who knows the meaning and does not rely solely on the wording it contains.

قاعدة ١٣ جواز الأخذ بما اتضح معناه من الأذكار والأدعية وإن لم يصح رواية

بساط الشريعة قاض بجواز الأخذ بما اتضح معناه من الأذكار والأدعية، وإن لم يصح رواية، كما نبه عليه ابن العربي في السراج وغيره.

وجاءت أحاديث في تأثير الدعاء الجاري على لسان العبد، المنبعث من همته، حتى أدخل مالك رحمه الله في موطئه في باب دعائه ﷺ قول أبي الدرداء:

(نامت العيون وهدأت الجفون ولم يبق إلا أنت يا حي يا قيوم).

وقال ﷺ للذي دعا بـ: (إني أسألك بأنك الله لا إله إلا أنت الأحد الصمد ..... الخ)، (لقد دعوت الله باسمه الأعظم).

وكذا قال للذي دعا بـ: (يا ودود، يا ودود، يا ذا العرش المجيد)، إلى غير ذلك.

فدل على أن كل واضح، مستحسن في ذاته، يحسن الأخذ به، سيما إن استند لأصل شرعي، كرؤيا صالح، أو إلهام ثابت المزية كأحزاب الشاذلي، والنووي، ونحوهما.

وفي أحزاب "ابن سبعين" كثير من المبهمات والموهمات، فَوَجَبَ التَّجَنُّبُ جملةً لمحل الخطر، إلا لعالم يعتبر المعنى ولا يتقيد باللفظ فيه.

Nevertheless, the prayers that are composed from (what has been related in) Hadiths are more perfect in their affair because there are no additions (to the Sunnah) in them except their composition. That is especially the case if they are taken from the recognized shaykhs. For instance, if a scholar investigated them exhaustively and completely, they would find that the majority of the supplications of al-Shādhilī are of this category, in addition to what they comprise of reminders and their being effective at bringing about desired matters in general. And Allah knows best.

والوظائف المجموعة من الأحاديث أكمل أمرًا، إذ لا زيادة فيها سوى الجمع سيما إن أخذت من المشايخ، وجل أحزاب الشاذلي عند التفصيل والنظر التام للعالم بالأحاديث من ذلك مع ما تضمنته من التذكير والتأثير بالأمور المطلوبة في الجملة، والله أعلم.

PRINCIPLE 14: RETREAT IS MORE SPECIFIC THAN SOLITUDE. AND IN ITS DIFFERENT KINDS AND FORMS, IT IS A KIND OF I'TIKĀF.

Retreat is more specific than solitude. In its different forms and categories, it does constitute a category of *i'tikāf*. However, it is not done inside a mosque (for the most part), though it may be performed there. For the most part, the people of the path have not assigned it a specific maximum limit, though the Sunnah indicates 40 days due to the appointment of Mūsā ﷺ.

However, in reality the most moderate way is 30 days because that is the original appointment. In addition, the Prophet ﷺ used to stay, in his retreat in Ḥirāʾ, for around a month, as recorded in Muslim.

Likewise, he would isolate himself from his womenfolk. And fasting is done for a single month. Furthermore, the growth of the Moon and its decrease is like the disciple in his wayfaring.

Its minimum period is 10 days, due to his ﷺ *i'tikāf* lasting for 10 days.[9]

For the complete saint, it is an increase in his state, while for others it is an ascension. And it is imperative that one have a standard upon which he depends.

The purpose of it is to cleanse the heart of the impurities that it has accumulated and to isolate the heart for solitary remembrance and a single reality.

However, if performed without a shaykh, it is dangerous.

While it has some great openings, it may not be appropriate for some individuals. Consequently, each person should take note of his state.

And Allah knows best.

---

(9) Meaning in the last ten days of Ramadan.

قاعدة ١٤ الخلوة أخص من العزلة وهو بوجوهها وصورتها نوع من الاعتكاف

الخلوة أخص من العزلة وهو بوجوهها وصورتها نوع من الاعتكاف، ولكن لا في المسجد، وربما كانت فيه، وأكثرها عند القوم لا حد له، لكن السنة تشير للأربعين؛ لمواعدة موسى عليه السلام.

والقصد في الحقيقة: الثلاثون، إذ هي أصل المواعدة، وجاور ﷺ لاعتكافه بحراء شهراً كما في مسلم.

وكذا اعتزل من نسائه، وشهر الصوم الواحد، وزيادة القمر ونقصانه كالمريد في سلوكه.

وأقلُّها عشرٌ لاعتكافه - عليه السلام - العشرَ، وهي للكامل زيادة في حاله، ولغيره ترقية، ولا بد من أصل يرجع إليه، والقصد بها تطهُّر القلب من أدناس الملابسة، وإفرادُ القلب لذكر واحد، وحقيقةٍ واحدة، ولكنها بلا شيخ مخطرة، ولها فتوحٌ عظيمة، وقد لا تصلح لأقوام، فليعتبر كلُّ أحد بها حاله، والله أعلم.

PRINCIPLE 15: THE LIGHTS OF INVOCATIONS BURNS THE TRAITS OF THE SLAVE.

The lights of invocations scorch the traits of the slave and cause heat in the soul by removing the latter from its nature. That is why prayer upon the Prophet ﷺ was ordered along with them, because it is like water such that it strengthens the soul and puts out the flame of its nature.

The secret in that is the prostration to Adam when they said: "And we glorify Your praise and declare Your holiness. He said: 'I know that which you do not know.'"

That is why the shaykhs ordered (the disciples to perform) prayer upon the Messenger of Allah ﷺ whenever they are overtaken by ecstasy and spiritual tasting.

This assertion has supporting evidence. And it is what al-Ṣiddīq[10] ؓ indicated when he said, "Prayer upon Muhammad ﷺ is more effective at erasing sins than cold water to fire…" Accordingly, upon that let the disciple depend.

In *Miftāḥ al-Falāḥ*, it was stated that the signs of the illumination is the sensation of heat in one's inner being.

And Allah knows best.

---

(10) Abū Bakr al-Ṣiddīq.

قاعدة ١٥ نورانية الأذكار محرقة لأوصاف العبد

نورانية الأذكار محرقة لأوصاف العبد، ومثيرة لحرارة نفسه بانحراف النفس عن طبعها، فمن ثم أمر بالصلاة على النبي ﷺ معها لأنها كالماء تقوي النفوس وتذهب وهج الطباع، وسر ذلك في السجود لآدم عند قولهم: ﴿وَنَحْنُ نُسَبِّحُ بِحَمْدِكَ وَنُقَدِّسُ لَكَ ۖ قَالَ إِنِّي أَعْلَمُ مَا لَا تَعْلَمُونَ ۝﴾. ولهذا أمر المشايخ بالصلاة على رسول الله ﷺ عند غلبة الوجد والذوق ولذلك شاهد، وقد أشار إليه الصديق رضي الله عنه إذ قال: (الصلاة على محمد ﷺ أمحق للذنوب من الماء البارد للنار ... الأثر إلى آخره) فليعتمد.

وقد نص في مفتاح الفلاح أن علامة الفتح، ثوران الحرارة في الباطن والله أعلم.

PRINCIPLE 16: UPHOLDING THE CONDITIONS IN THAT FOR WHICH THEY ARE CONDITIONS IS IMPERATIVE FOR THE SEEKER.

It is imperative that the seeker maintain the conditions for the validity of what he is performing. Otherwise, his performance of the act is not valid, even if he has done it in form.

And the conditions of remembrance which have been stipulated for its gathering are three:

1. That the time (in which the gathering takes place) is free of any obligation or emphasized recommendation which may be negatively affected by his act. Examples include if he were to stay awake and then sleep through the prayer (time), that he should find it difficult to perform, that he should neglect his litany, harm his family, and so on.

2. That the gathering is free of anything unlawful or detestable within it, such as hearing women's voices, their attendance, or the presence of heretical folk who should be avoided, or to intentionally serve food by which nearness is not sought, or about whose lawfulness there is even the slightest doubt. The same rule applies if the gathering is done on an unlawful material, such as silk or the like, or is involved with the mention of evil people or the preoccupation with false rumours.

3. Adhering to the etiquette of remembrance, such as it being legislated or comparable, whereby it is done with utterances that are clear and valid. It also means that it is recited with tranquillity, even if one alternates between standing and sitting. However, one should avoid swaying, shouting, and the like, for that is from the acts of the insane. This was indicated by Mālik ؓ when he was asked about people who perform that, for he responded by saying: "Are they insane?"

At best, it is detestable in a way that it is more appropriate to forbid it. Understand!

And Allah knows best.

قاعدة 16 مراعاة الشروط في مشروطها لازم لمريدها

مراعاة الشروط في مشروطها لازم لمريده، وإلا لم يصح وجوده له، وإن قامت صورته.

وشروط الذكر التي تتعين عند الجمع له ثلاث:

أولها: خلو الوقت عن واجب أو مندوب متأكد يلزم من عمله الإخلال به، كأن يسهر فينام عن الصلاة، أو يتثاقل فيها، أو يفرط في ورده، أو يضر بأهله، إلى غير ذلك.

ثانيهما: خلوه عن محرم أو مكروه يقترن به كإسماع النساء وحضورهن أو حضور مَنْ يُتَّقَى من الأحداث، أو قصد طعام لا قربة فيه، أو داخلته شبهة ولو قلت، أو فراش محرم كحرير ونحوه، أو ذكر مساوئ الناس، أو الاشتغال بالأراجيف إلى غير ذلك.

ثالثها: التزام أدب الذكر من كونه شرعيا أو في معناه، بحيث يكون بما صح واتضح وذكره على وجه السكينة، وإن مع قيام مرة وقعود أخرى، لا مع رقص وصياح ونحوه، فإنه من فعل المجانين كما أشار مالك رحمه الله، لما سئل عنهم فقال: (أمجانين هم). وغاية كلامه الاستقباح بوجه يكون المنع فيه أحرى فافهم، والله أعلم.

PRINCIPLE 17: THE INVOCATIONS THAT ARE RELATED TO WORLDLY AFFAIRS LEAD TO LOVE OF ALLAH AND ATTACHMENT TO HIS REMEMBRANCE.

Souls can be lured – through their natural inclinations – towards that in which there is legislated religious benefit. That is why invocations and acts of worship for worldly benefits have been encouraged, such as the recitation of Sūrah al-Wāqiʿah to ward off poverty, بِسْمِ اللهِ الَّذِي لَا يَضُرُّ مَعَ اسْمِهِ شَيْءٌ فِي الأَرْضِ وَلَا فِي السَّمَاءِ وَهُوَ السَّمِيعُ العَلِيمُ (In the name of Allah with Whose name nothing can cause harm in the heavens and the Earth and He is the All-Hearing, the All-Knowing) for the sake of warding off sudden afflictions, أَعُوذُ بِكَلِمَاتِ اللهِ التَّامَّةِ مِنْ شَرِّ مَا خَلَقَ (I seek refuge in the perfect words of Allah from the evil of what He has created) to ward off the harm of poisonous animals and protection of one's home, and other such prayers such as supplications to ward off debt and to help one obtain means, including wealth, honour, and so on.

The explanation of this principle is that if one receives exactly what is sought, it will cause him to love it. Thenceforward, loving it will cause him to love the one Who has come with it and to Whom it is attributed in principle and in ruling. Thus, they lead to the love of Allah. And if he does not obtain his ultimate objective, the gentle mercy is nevertheless found in it, such that at the very least, the soul will become attached to the remembrance of the Real. And instilling that value – by way of its nature – is more possible and feasible.

It is in light of this standard that Shaykh Abū al-ʿAbbās al-Būnī – and others who followed similar methods – based himself in mentioning the names and their special qualities. Otherwise, the foundation is not actually found in making invocations and acts of obedience a means for obtaining worldly objectives, out of veneration for such acts.

And Allah knows best.

قاعدة ١٧ الأذكار التي تتعلق بالأمور الدنيوية تؤدي إلى حب الله والأنس بذكره

استراق النفوس بملائمها طبعا، لما فيه نفع ديني مشروع، فمن ثم رغب في أذكار وعبادات لأمور دنيوية، كقراءة سورة الواقعة لدفع الفاقة: و(بِسْمِ اللهِ الَّذِي لَا يَضُرُّ مَعَ اسْمِهِ شَيْءٌ فِي الْأَرْضِ وَلَا فِي السَّمَاءِ وَهُوَ السَّمِيعُ الْعَلِيمُ) لصرف البلايا المفاجئة، و(أَعُوذُ بِكَلِمَاتِ اللهِ التَّامَّةِ مِنْ شَرِّ مَا خَلَقَ) لصرف شر ذوات السموم، والحفظ في المنزل، إلى غير ذلك من أذكار صرف الهموم والديون والإعانة على الأسباب، كالغنى والعز ونحوه.

بيان ذلك أنها إن أفادت عين ما قصدت له، كان داعيا لحبها، ثم حبها داع لحب من جاء بها، ومن نسبت له أصلا وفرعا، فهي مؤدية لحب الله، وإن لم تؤد ما قصدت له، فاللطف موجود بها، ولا أقل من أنس النفس بذكر الحق، ودخول ذلك من حيث الطباع أمكن وأيسر.

ولهذا الأصل استند الشيخ أبو العباس البوني ومن نحا نحوه في ذكر الأسماء وخواصها، وإلا فالأصل أن لا تجعل الأذكار والعبادات سببا في الأغراض الدنيوية إجلالا لها، والله أعلم.

PRINCIPLE 18: THE SPECIAL QUALITY OF EACH NAME OR INVOCATION IS IN ITS MEANING. ITS SECRET IS IN ITS NUMBER. AND THE RESPONSE FOR IT IS DEPENDENT UPON THE ASPIRATION OF ITS INVOKER.

The special quality of every name or invocation rests in its meaning, and its effect is found in its implication. Its secret is in its number, and the reception of a response to it depends on the level of aspiration found in its invoker.

For that reason, the scholar only benefits from invocations whose meanings are apparent and clear, while the ignoramus only benefits from invocations whose meanings are concealed or undetermined. And those between the two remain between the two.

It is imperative to adhere to the numbers established through legislation or derived through calculation because success depends upon that, as is the custom of Allah.

As for writing (in sand) and excessive reliance upon geometric figures, it is something derived from the science of humours and temperaments. And the remoteness of that science from the truth and success is quite evident. That is why Ibn al-Bannā ﷺ said, "Keep away from al-Būnī and his geometric shapes. And adhere to the best of examples and its likes." Al-Ḥātimī ﷺ said, "The science of letters is a noble science. However, it is blameworthy both in worldly and religious terms." Know this, and with Allah ﷺ is all success.

I say: As for its religious blameworthiness, it is due to its practitioner being immersed in unverified means, as opposed to proven ones. It diminishes one's standing in the station of reliance (upon God) owing to its excessive concentration on secondary means, just like undertaking cauterization in medicine. Additionally, it is from the foolhardiness of the soul and means of hastening relief.

قاعدة ١٨ كل اسم أو ذكر فخاصيته من معناه، وسره في عدده وإجابته على قدر همة صاحبه

كل اسم أو ذكر فخاصيته من معناه وتصريفه في مقتضاه، وسره في عدده وإجابته على قدر همة صاحبه، فمن ثم لا ينتفع عالم إلا بجلي واضح المعنى، ولا جاهل إلا بخفي لا يعرف معناه ويبقى من بينهما بينهما.

ولزم اعتبار العدد الموضوع شرعا، والمستخرج استنباطا لتوقف التحقيق عليه حسب سنة الله.

فأمَّا الكَتْبُ والتفريط في الشكل ونحوه، فأمرٌ مستفادٌ من علم الطباع والطبائع، ولا يخفى بعده عن الحق والتحقيق، فلذا قال ابن البنا رَضِيَ اللهُ عَنْهُ :

(باين البوني وأشكاله، ووافق خيرا النساج وأمثاله).

وقال الحاتمي رحمه الله:

(علم الحروف علم شريف لكنه مذموم دينا ودنيا). فاعلم ذلك، وبالله سبحانه التوفيق.

قلتُ: أما دينا، فلتوغل صاحبه في الأسباب المتوهمة دون المحققة، وذلك قادح في مقام التوكل؛ باعتبار الاجتهاد في المسبب، كالمبادرة

As for its blameworthiness in the world, it is because it comprises being preoccupied with a building of shoddy workmanship.

And Allah ﷻ knows best.

بالكَيِّ في التطبب؛ لأنه من نزق النفس واستعجال البرء فافهم.

وأما دنيا: فلأنه شغلٌ في وجه يخل بعمارتها. والله سبحانه أعلم.

PRINCIPLE 19: THE SAMĀʿ IS A DISPENSATION WITH THE SUFIS WHICH IS ALLOWED DUE TO NEED.

For a man to believe that something constitutes an act of drawing near when it actually is not is a heretical innovation. The same upshot applies for the one inventing a ruling that has no precedent. All of that is misguidance unless it can be traced back to a principle from which it is derived; in the latter case, its ruling would return to that.

There is no evidence whatsoever of the praiseworthiness of the *samāʿ*, if it is in fact permissible, despite the detailed rulings that the people of the path have given. The reality is that if it is permitted, then it is only a dispensation that has been allowed either in general or due to a need. As such, its conditions must be kept in mind, or else it should not be permitted.

And Allah knows best.

قاعدة 19 السماع عند الصوفية رخصة تباح لضرورة

اعتقاد المرء فيما ليس بقربة قربةً بدعةٌ، وكذا إحداثُ حكمٍ لم يتقدم، وكل ذلك ضلالٌ إلا أن يُرجَع لأصل استنبط منه، فيرجع حكمه إليه.

والسماع لا دلالة على ندبه عند مبيحه جملة، وإن وقع فيه تفصيل عند قوم، فالتحقيق أنه عند مبيحه رخصة تباح للضرورة، أو في الجملة، فيعتبر شرطُها وإلا فالمنع، والله أعلم.

PRINCIPLE 20: WHOEVER LISTENS BY WAY OF REALITY WILL OBTAIN REALIZATION. WHOEVER LISTENS BY WAY OF THE EGO WILL ONLY GAIN A WORSE STATE.

The capacity for acceptance is in accordance with the level of one's listening to what is said. Thus, whoever listens by way of reality will gain confirmation, while the one who listens through the ego will only worsen his state. If a person's listening is with the physical senses, his benefit will be restricted to the time of his listening.

From this perspective, the seeker of knowledge is not elevated in any affair of this world except that he is increased in his aversion to the truth. Similarly, the majority of people do not benefit from general gatherings, such as schools or social arrangements, except for the mere enjoyment of the moment. However, the person of realization benefits from what is stated from whatever direction it comes. Understand this well. And Allah knows best.

قاعدة ٢٠ من كان استماعه بالحقيقة استفاد التحقيق، ومن كان استماعه بالنفس استفاد سوء الحال

التهيؤ للقبول، على قدر الإصغاء للمقول، فمن كان استماعه بالحقيقة استفاد التحقق، ومن كان استماعه بالنفس استفاد سوء الحال، ومن كان سماعه بالطبع اقتصر نفعه على وقته، فمن ثم لا يزداد طالب العلم للدنيا مسألة إلا ازداد إدبارا عن الحق، ولا يستفيد غالب الناس من المحافل العامة، كالكُتَّاب والميعاد ونحوه، إلا استحلاؤه في الوقت. وينفع ذا الحقيقة ما يفيد من أي وجه خرج، فافهم، والله أعلم.

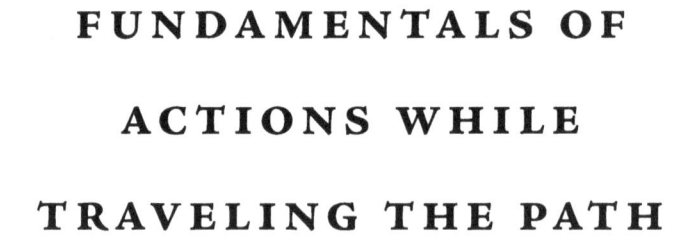

FUNDAMENTALS OF ACTIONS WHILE TRAVELING THE PATH

ضوابط العمل في السلوك

PRINCIPLE 21: KNOWLEDGE IS A PRECONDITION FOR ACTION.

It is incorrect to act upon anything before knowing its ruling and its consequence. Thus, the statement of someone who says, "I will not learn until I (first) act" is like one how says, "I will not seek treatment until my ailment departs." Such a person will neither seek treatment, nor will his ailment leave him. However, the correct order is knowledge, then action, then divulgation and then benefiting.

And from Allah alone comes success.

قاعدة 21 شرط العلم للعمل

لا يصلح العمل بالشيء إلا بعد معرفة حكمه ووجهه، فقول القائل: ''لا أتعلم حتى أعمل'' كقوله: ''لا أتداوى حتى تذهب علتي''، فهو لا يتداوى ولا تذهب علته، ولكن العلم ثم العمل ثم النشر والإفادة، وبالله التوفيق.

PRINCIPLE 22: CORRECTING ONE'S MANNER OF SEEKING ASSISTS ONE IN ATTAINING WHAT HE IS SEEKING.

Correcting one's manner of seeking facilitates one's realization of what he is seeking. It is from this viewpoint that asking excellent questions is deemed half of knowledge, because the response that a questioner will receive is according to the refinement of his question.

Ibn ʿArīf ﷺ said, "Every true seeker of knowledge must have three things:
1. Knowledge of impartiality and adherence to its specifications.
2. Perfecting his manner of asking questions, purging them of every type of ambiguity.
3. Knowing well the difference between conflict (*khilāf*) and difference of opinion (*ikhtilāf*)."

I say: That which returns to a single principle is termed *ikhtilāf*. The ruling of Allah for each individual will return to what Allah has granted him in his reasoning.[11] That which returns to two different principles, in which one of the two may be disproven after thorough investigation, is termed *khilāf*.

And Allah knows best.

---

(11) Translator's note: This is to say that the ruling of Allah regarding a particular issue – which is governed by a single principle – will be determined by each individual capable of independent reasoning, in accordance with the capacity that Allah has given him.

قاعدة ٢٢ إحكام وجه الطلب معين على تحصيل المطلوب

إحكام وجه الطلب معين على تحصيل المطلوب، فإن ثم كان حسن السؤال نصف العلم، إذ إجابة السائل على قدر تهذيب المسائل.

وقد قال ابن العريف رحمه الله: (لا بد لكلّ طالب علم حقيقيٍ من ثلاثة أشياء:

أحدها: معرفة الإنصاف، ولزومه بالأوصاف.

الثاني: تحرير وجه السؤال، وتجريده من عموم جهات الإشكال.

الثالث: تحقيق الفرق بين الخلاف والاختلاف).

قلت: فما رجع لأصل واحد فاختلاف، يكون حكم الله في كلّ ما أدّاه الله إليه اجتهاده، وما رجع لأصلين يتبين بطلان أحدهما عند تحقيق النظر فخلاف، والله أعلم.

PRINCIPLE 23: PERFECTION OF WORSHIP IS BY UPHOLDING ITS EXTERNAL AND INTERNAL LIMITS WITHOUT EXCESS OR LAXITY.

Worship is perfected by preserving it and persevering upon it. That is accomplished by maintaining its external and internal limits without excess or laxity. The person who is lax will neglect it while the person of excess innovates, regardless of whether or not he deems his excess as a means of drawing near.

From this standpoint, it is said, "Misgivings are an innovation whose origin is ignorance of the Sunnah or mental deficiency." It is dispelled through the constant invocation of سُبْحَانَ الْمَلِكِ الْخَلَّاقِ (Blessed is the King, the Creator of all) and إِنْ يَشَأْ يُذْهِبْكُمْ وَيَأْتِ بِخَلْقٍ جَدِيدٍ وَمَا ذَلِكَ عَلَى اللهِ بِعَزِيزٍ (If He willed, He would do away with you and bring a new creation. And that is not difficult for Allah)[12] along with every litany. Yet another of its origins is excessive attachment to laxity and taking dispensations from the statements of the scholars, which has been negated by the statement, "Do not seek out every dispensation, because that is misguidance by consensus of the scholars." Understand this well.

---

(12) *Fāṭir*, 16-17.

قاعدة 23 كمال العبادة بإقامة حدودها الظاهرة والباطنة ومن غير غلو ولا تفريط

كمال العبادة بحفظها والمحافظة عليها، وذلك بإقامة حدودها الظاهرة والباطنة من غير غلو ولا تفريط، فالمفرط مضيّع، والغالي مبتدع، سيما إن اعتقد القربة في زيادته، فمن ثم قيل: الوسوسة بدعة، وأصلها جهل بالسنة، أو خبال في العقل يدفعها دوام ذكر (سبحان الملك الخلاق) ﴿إِن يَشَأْ يُذْهِبْكُمْ وَيَأْتِ بِخَلْقٍ جَدِيدٍ ۝ وَمَا ذَٰلِكَ عَلَى ٱللَّهِ بِعَزِيزٍ ۝﴾. مع كل ورد، والتزام التلهي والأخذ بالرخص من أقوال العلماء النافية لها لا تتبع الرخص فإنها ضلال بإجماع فافهم.

PRINCIPLE 24: THE ORIGIN OF EVERY GOOD OR EVIL: MORSELS AND ASSOCIATION.

The source of every good or evil is in morsels and association. Consequently, whatever you will, your actions will reflect that. And accompany whomever you will, for you are upon that person's conviction. It has been said that whatever is eaten in negligence will also be used in negligence.

That is why some of the people of the path considered it preferable to recite the name of Allah over every morsel that they consumed and to praise Him for it after swallowing. However, Ibn al-Ḥājj said, "That is fine. However, the Sunnah is to recite the name of Allah at the beginning and to praise Allah at the end, without any addition. And the Sunnah is better."

I mentioned this to one of the people of good, but he accepted it. However, there still remained within me some doubt about it. So, I spoke to him again about it and said to him, "It contradicts the Sunnah of the Hadith about eating." He said, "That is if he is eating with others." So, I accepted his deliberation.

Thus, it became clear to me. So, I recanted from my acceptance of it, limiting myself to the Sunnah, making it a judge of all customs, from whomever they emerge and in whatever state. And Allah knows best.

قاعدة ٢٤ أصل كل خير وشر: اللقمة والخلطة

أصل كل خير وشر اللقمة والخلطة، فَكُلْ ما شئتَ فمثله تفعل، واصحب من شئتَ فأنت على دينه.

قيل: وما أكل بالغفلة استعمل فيها، فاستحبوا لذلك أن يُسَمِّي على كل لقمة ويحمد على بلعها.

قال ابن الحاج: وهذا حسن، ولكن السنة التسمية أولا، والحمدلة آخرا من غير زائد، والسنة أحسن.

فذكرتُ ذلك لبعض أهل الخير، فقبله، وبقي في نفسي شيء منه، فرددت الكلام معه فيه وقلت: هو معارض لسنة الحديث على الطعام، فقال: هذا إن كان معه أحد، فقبلت بحثه.

ثم بدا لي فرجعت عن قبوله توقفا مع السنة، وإجراءها الحكم على الاعتياد في حق كل أحد على كل حال. والله أعلم.

PRINCIPLE 25: LET NONE OF YOU BE LIKE THE BAD SLAVE, WHO, IF HE IS NOT MADE TO FEAR, DOES NOT WORK.

Reverence of what Allah has made venerable is sought. And having contempt for it may even be disbelief. Thus, the words of those who say, "We have not worshipped Him out of fear of His Fire, nor desirous of His Paradise," are not valid without qualification. That is because it is either:

1) Disdain for them both, when Allah ﷻ has made them venerable; it is impermissible for a Muslim to have contempt for them.

2) Or it comprises considering oneself free of need of them both, while no believer is free from needing the blessing of his Lord.

Yes, it is true that they did not make them the objectives of their worship. Rather, they worshipped Allah not for the sake of anything else. And they sought Paradise and salvation from the Fire, but not through any act of theirs. The evidence of that is found in His ﷻ words, "We only feed you for the sake of Allah. We want from you neither reward nor gratitude."[13] They thus made the reason for their action the desire for the Countenance of Allah ﷻ. They mentioned their fear and hope afterwards, independent of that.

And Allah ﷻ revealed to Dāwūd ﷺ, "Who does more wrong than the one who worships Me out of fear of My Fire or desirous of My Paradise? If I had not created Paradise or the Fire, would I not be worthy of being obeyed?"

And in a narrated report, it states: "Let not one of you be like the bad slave. If he is not made to fear, he does not work. Nor

---

(13) *al-Insān*, 9.

قاعدة 25 لا يكن أحدكم كالعبد السوء، إن لم يخف لم يعمل

تعظيم ما عظم الله متعين، واحتقار ذلك ربما كان كفرا، فلا يصح فهم قولهم: (ما عبدناه خوفا من ناره، ولا طمعا في جنته) على الإطلاق؛ لأنه إما احتقار لهما وقد عظمهما الله تعالى، فلا يصح احتقارهما من مسلم، وإما استغناء عنهما، ولا غنى لمؤمن عن بركة مولاه.

نعم لم يتصدوهما بالعبادة، بل عملوا لله لا لشيء، وطلبوا منه الجنة والنجاة من النار، لا بشيء، وشاهد ذلك في قوله تعالى: ﴿إِنَّمَا نُطْعِمُكُمْ لِوَجْهِ ٱللَّهِ لَا نُرِيدُ مِنكُمْ جَزَآءً وَلَا شُكُورًا ۝﴾ الآية، إذ جعلوا علة العمل إرادة وجه الله تعالى، ثم ذكروا خوفهم ورجاءهم مجردين عن ذلك بعد.

وقد أوحى الله تعالى إلى داود عليه السلام: (ومن أظلم ممن عبدني خوفا من ناري، أو طمعا في جنتي، لو لم أخلق جنة ولا نارا ألم أكن أهلا أن أطاع).

وفي الخبر: (لا يكن أحدكم كالعبد السوء، إن لم يخف لم يعمل، ولا كالأجير السوء، إن لم يعط الأجرة لم يعمل).

وقال عمر رضي الله عنه، ويروى مرفوعا: (نعم العبد صهيب لو لم يخف الله لم يعصه).

be like the bad worker. If he is not paid, he does not work."

'Umar ؓ said, "How excellent of a slave is Ṣuhayb. If he were to have nothing to fear from Allah, he does not disobey Him." This has also been narrated as a Prophetic Hadith. The implication of this is that even if he has no fear of Allah, he will never disobey him. Thus, his motivation for abandoning disobedience is not out of fear nor hope, love nor life, reverence nor fright, nor anything else. And Allah knows best.

يعني: أنه لا يخاف الله، ولا يعصيه.

فالحامل له على ترك المعصية غير الخوف من رجاء أو حب أو حياء أو هيبة أو خشية، إلى غير ذلك.

والله أعلم.

FUNDAMENTAL KNOWLEDGE FOR THE WAYFARER

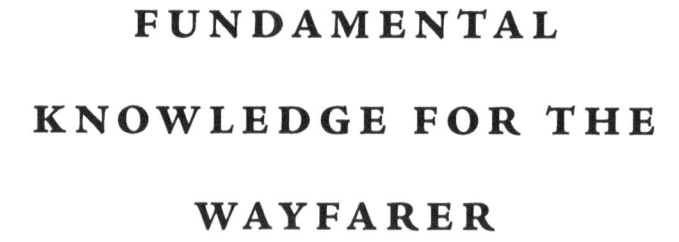

ضوابط العلم للسالك

PRINCIPLE 26: THERE BEING VARIOUS KINDS OF GOOD INDICATES THE EXISTENCE OF A VARIETY OF APPROACHES TO GOOD.

The existence of various categories of good indicates the existence of a variety of approaches to good. This requires the achievement of good by every person who approaches good.

For that reason, each group has a path. The *taṣawwuf* of the ordinary folk is what is contained in the books of al-Muḥāsibī and scholars that adopted his approach. The *taṣawwuf* of the jurist is the *taṣawwuf* which Ibn al-Ḥājj advocated for in his *al-Madkhal*. For the scholar of Hadith, there is the *taṣawwuf* which Ibn al-ʿArabī concentrated on in his *al-Sirāj*. For the worshipper, there is the *taṣawwuf* around which al-Ghazālī revolved in his *al-Manhāj*. For the adherent to spiritual practices, there is the *taṣawwuf* that al-Qushayrī indicated in his *al-Risālah*. For the ascetic, there is the *taṣawwuf* encompassed in *al-Qūt* and *al-Iḥyāʾ*. For the sage, there is the *taṣawwuf* that al-Ḥātimī included in his books. For the logician, there is the *taṣawwuf* put forth by Ibn Sabʿīn in his works. And for the humorist, there is the *taṣawwuf* that al-Būnī introduced in his *Asrār*. For the scholar of the fundamentals of religion, there is the *taṣawwuf* that al-Shādhilī erected in his research.

As such, each one should be sought in its proper place. And from Allah is all success.

قاعدة 26 تعدد وجوه الحسن، يقضي بتعدد الاستحسان

تعدد وجوه الحسن يقضي بتعدد الاستحسان [وحصول الحسن لكل مستحسن]، فمن ثم كان لكل فريق طريق: فللعامي تصوف حوته كتب المحاسبي، ومن نحا نحوه، وللفقيه تصوف رامه ابن الحاج في مدخله، وللمحدث تصوف حام حوله ابن العربي في سراجه، وللعابد تصوف دار عليه الغزالي في منهاجه، وللمتريض تصوف نبه عليه القشيري في رسالته، وللناسك تصوف حواه القوت والإحياء، وللحكيم تصوف أدخله الحاتمي في كتبه، وللمنطقي تصوف نحا إليه ابن سبعين في تآليفه، وللطبائعي تصوف جاء به البوني في أسراره، وللأصولي تصوف قام الشاذلي بتحقيقه، فليعتبر كل بأصله من محله، وبالله التوفيق.

PRINCIPLE 27: EACH SCIENCE IS ONLY TAKEN FROM THOSE WHO DOMINATE IT.

Each science is only taken from its experts. Thus, a Sufi is not relied upon in jurisprudence, unless it is known that he has mastered it. Nor is a jurist relied upon in *taṣawwuf*, unless he is known for his mastery in it. And a scholar of Hadith is not relied upon in either of them unless he is known to have mastered them.

Thus, it is necessary for the Sufi aspirant to seek jurisprudence from the jurists. And he only refers to the people of the Path in that which concerns the rectification of his inner being.

That is why Shaykh Abū Muhammad al-Marjānī ﷺ used to order his companions to refer to the legal jurists in questions of jurisprudence, even if he knew their answers.

Understand well!

قاعدة 27 إنما يؤخذ علم كل شيء من أربابه

إنما يؤخذ علم كل شيء من أربابه، فلا يعتمد صوفي في الفقه، إلا أن يعرف قيامه عليه، ولا فقيه في التصوف، إلا أن يعرف تحقيقه له، ولا محدث فيهما، إلا أن يعلم قيامه بهما.

فلزم طلب الفقه من قبل الفقهاء لمريد التصوف، وإنما يرجع لأهل الطريق فيما يختص بصلاح باطنه من ذلك، ومن غيره.

ولذلك كان الشيخ أبو محمد المرجاني رضي الله عنه، يأمر أصحابه بالرجوع للفقهاء في مسائل الفقه، وإن كان عارفًا بها، فافهم.

PRINCIPLE 28: WHATEVER EMERGES FROM THE HEART ENTERS THE HEART, WHILE WHATEVER IS LIMITED TO THE TONGUE WILL NOT TRAVERSE THE EARS.

Whatever emerges from the heart enters the heart, while whatever is limited to the tongue will not traverse the ears.

Thereafter, if it enters the heart, it will either be met by an impediment such that it will be pushed away by rejection, as is the state of the disbelievers, or by turning away, similar to the condition of the hypocrites. Or, a thin barrier will lie between it and its direct contact with the heart, as is observed in the states of disobedience. Or, it will touch its innermost part and reach its reality, causing one to either act upon it or refrain from it based on its dictates. And this is the state of the people of truth among the disciples.

As for the Knower (ʿĀrif), he benefits from anyone that provides benefit, whether it emerges from the heart or otherwise.

قاعدة 28 ما خرج من القلب، دخل للقلب، وما قصر على اللسان لم يجاوز الآذان

ما خرج من القلب دخل للقلب، وما قصر على اللسان لم يجاوز الآذان، ثم هو بعد دخوله القلب إما أن يلقى معارضا فيدفعه بجحود كحال الكفار، أو بإعراض كأحوال المنافقين، أو يحول بينه وبين مباشرة القلب حائل رقيق كأحوال العصاة، أو يمس سويداءه، ويباشر حقيقته فيوجب الإقدام والإحجام على حكمه، كحال أهل الحق من المريدين، فأما العارف فيستفيد من كل ذي فائدة، كان من قلب أو غيره، فافهم.

PRINCIPLE 29: DISTINCTIONS DO NOT NECESSITATE SUPERIORITY.

Distinctions do not logically require superiority. And it is only permitted to follow someone with perfect knowledge and religion.

If it were said that superiority is designated by distinctions, it would necessitate considering Iblīs superior to the generality of believers, because he enjoys the distinction of moving more swiftly than the wind, walking upon water, traversing the Earth in an instant, and the fact that he and his tribe see us, from where we do not see him.

It would also necessitate considering al-Khiḍr as superior to Mūsā ﷺ, despite this being untrue.

Thus, it follows that superiority is wholly earned and assigned through the decree of Allah. Consequently, no challenge is to be made regarding it except through a revelatory text that has been confirmed in its category. However, when there is evidence, a form of probabilistic superiority can be established.

As such, it is imperative to refrain from absolute declarations (of superiority), while it is permitted to engage in declaring (probabilistic) superiority in situations where it is needed. Otherwise, abstaining from speaking on it is superior.

And Allah knows best.

قاعدة ٢٩ المزية لا تقتضي التفضيل

المزية لا تقتضي التفضيل، والاقتداء لا يصح إلا بذي علم كامل ودين.

ولو قيل بالتفضيل بالمزايا للزم تفضيل إبليس على عوام المؤمنين، إذ له مزية خرق الهواء، والمشي على الماء، ونفوذ الأرض في لحظة، وما أثبت الله له تعالى من أنه يرانا هو وقبيله من حيث لا نراه.

وللزم تفضيل الخضر على موسى عليهما السلام، وكل ذلك لا يصح.

فلزم أن التفضيل بحكم الله في الجملة فلا يتعرض له إلا بتوقيف ثابت في بابه، ولكن للدليل ترجيح فوجب التوقف عن الجزم، وجاز الخوض في الترجيح إذا أحوج إليه الوقت، وإلا فترك الكلام فيه أولى والله أعلم.

PRINCIPLE 30: SPEAKING SURELY ABOUT THE BELIEF OF A MUSLIM ON THE SAINTHOOD OF A PIOUS PERSON.

Evidence may drive a certain supposition until it reaches the level of surety, even if it is not treated as such in all possible cases. An example of this phenomenon is the certain belief in the piety of a Muslim from whom the signs of Islam have manifested, or in the sainthood whose actions, words, witnessed feats and states indicate his station.

However, this is judged through our (limited) knowledge, such that we do not declare with certainty what Allah knows about the person, except regarding those whom some special quality has come to us from Him, such as the ten who were promised Paradise.

It has been authentically narrated, "If you witness a man being attached to the *masjid*, bear witness to his faith." It has also been authentically narrated, "Two qualities are not joined in a hypocrite: excellent conduct and sound understanding of the religion. And two qualities are not joined in a believer: miserliness and evil conduct."

The swearing of Saʿd to the belief of a man has also been authentically narrated. And the Messenger of Allah ﷺ did not criticize his oath, even if he responded by saying, "Or a Muslim".

The Hadith, "There are three characteristics that, if they exist together in a person, he is a hypocrite …" is also authentic.

However, this Hadith does not apply to every believer who incurs such actions without any exception. Rather, it is applied to the one who is indifferent to the states in which he incurs them, such as contracts, actions, or statements, as evidenced by his words, "When he…" about each of those circumstances.

This is corroborated by his ﷺ statement, "A believer may have, by nature, any characteristic except treachery and lying."

He negated from him the nature of lying, but not that he

قاعدة ٣٠ القطع بإيمان مسلم أو ولاية صالح

قد تفيد الدلائل من الظن ما يتنزل منزلة القطع، وإن كان لا يجرى على حكمه في جميع الوجوه، كالقطع بإيمان مسلم ظهرت منه أعلام الإسلام، وكولاية صالح دلت على مقامه أفعاله وأقواله وشواهد أحواله، كل ذلك في علمنا من غير جزم بعلم الله فيه، إلا في حق من جاءنا عن الله مخصص له، كالعشرة المشهود لهم بالجنة.

وقد صح: (إذا رأيتم الرجل يعتاد المسجد، فاشهدوا له بالإيمان).

وصح: (خصلتان لا يجتمعان في منافق: حسن سمت، وفقه دين، وخصلتان لا تجتمعان في مؤمن: البخل، وسوء الخلق).

وصح حلف سعد على إيمان رجل، فلم ينكر عليه رسول الله ﷺ يمينه وإن رده بقول: أو مسلم.

وصح: (ثلاثة من كُنَّ فيه فهو منافق) الحديث.

ولا يتناول من واقع ذلك من المؤمنين جملة، بل مجراه في حق من لا يبالي في أي جزء وقعت منه تلك الخصال من عقد أو عمل أو قول، بدليل قوله ''إذا'' في كل واحدة.

ويشهد لذلك قوله ﷺ: (كل الخصال يطبع عليها المؤمن ليس الخيانة والكذب).

would not lie. Thus, if it occurs from him, it is a transient trait and not from his nature, which is different from the hypocrite.

For that reason, such characteristics do not affect the believer in all his circumstances, since he will avoid them in one or more situations, even if it is just his faith and his belief in Divine Oneness. This is different from the hypocrite, who is never exempted from it in any situation, even when it comes to disbelief, because such characteristics are not limited to his exterior actions. Rather, they exist in his inner reality, unlike others. And Allah knows best.

These words (in the Hadith) may refer to a trait of hypocrisy that is lower than pure hypocrisy, which is an interpretation championed by a group of scholars.

And Allah knows best.

فنفى عنه أن يكون مطبوعا عليها لا غيره، فهي وإن وقعت منه فبالعرض لا بالإصالة، بخلاف المنافق، ولذلك لم تصح من مؤمن في كل شيء، إذ يستثني جزءا، ولو الإيمان والتوحيد، بخلاف المنافق فإنه لا يستثني جزءا ولو في باب الكفر؛ إذ لا يجزم به ظاهرا كغيره، فكانت فيه لا في غيره. والله أعلم.

وقد يريد نفاقًا دون نفاق، وحمله عليه جماعة من العلماء، والله أعلم.

PRINCIPLE 31: THE TONGUES OF CREATION ARE THE PENS OF THE REAL.

The tongues of creation are the pens of the Real. As such, their praising of a person in a way that pleases the Real is, in fact, the praise of the Real for that person. For if that for which he is praised is really his state, then that praise is a blessing. If not, it is an encouragement and praise. If he is thankful and renders himself worthy of such praise, then Allah will perfect it for him and increase him in it. If not, then it will be removed from him.

What is taken into account in this regard is the general attitude of the masses towards that person, and what their souls feel for him. This is opposed to any criticism and denial levelled against him whose falsehood is indicated by the lack of status and esteem that the author of such criticism enjoys within the general public. It is also proven false by the malicious agitation of the one who makes the impugning statement. The latter is revealed by what removes the cause of criticism, such as death and the like.

It has also been authentically narrated, "When Allah loves a slave, He calls Jibrīl…"

Thus, love is known by the acceptance that one receives when he is met. Otherwise, the transient quality does not elevate the reality.

Understand well.

قاعدة ٣١ ألسنة الخلق، أقلام الحق

ألسنة الخلق أقلام الحق، فثناؤهم عليه بما يرتضيه الحق ثناء من الحق عليه بذلك. فإن كان فيه فالثناء منة، وإلا فهو تنبيه وثناء، إن شكره بالقيام بحقه أتمه عليه وزاده منه وإلا سلبه عنه. والمعتبر الإطلاق العام وما في النفوس لا ما يقع من الطعن بالجحود الذي يدل على بطلانه فقدان الترجمة في المترجم، واضطراب القائل في قوله، ويظهر ذلك بارتفاع موجب النكير كالموت ونحوه.

وقد صح: (إن الله إذا أحب عبدا نادى جبريل) الحديث.

فيعتبر الحب بالقبول عند اللقاء ونحوه، وإلا فالعارض لا يرفع الحقيقة، فافهم.

PRINCIPLE 32: PRECAUTION REGARDING THE BOOK TALBĪS IBLĪS, AL-FUTŪḤĀT, AND OTHERS.

The people of religious counsel have recommended (the books) *al-Talbīs* of Ibn al-Jawzī, *al-Futūḥāt* of al-Ḥātimī – and indeed all or the majority of his books, the books of Ibn Sabʿīn, Ibn al-Fāriḍ, Ibn Ahlā, Ibn Sudkīn, al-ʿAfīf al-Tilimsānī, al-Īkī al-ʿAjamī, al-Aswad al-Aqṭaʿ, Abū Isḥāq al-Tujaymī, al-Shushtarī, and some parts of *al-Iḥyā'* – most of which are in the section on destructive traits, as well as his *al-Nafkh* and *al-Taswiyah*. However, they encouraged keeping such books away from those who are not worthy of them.

Also included are al-Ghazālī's *Miʿrāj al-Sālikīn* and *al-Munqidh* and some sections of *Qūt al-Qulūb* of Abū Ṭālib al-Makkī and the books of al-Suhrawardī and his peers.

However, the precaution applies to the places where self-deception may occur. It does not mean that they should be avoided altogether. For the main reference point is knowledge.

And the latter is only completed by three characteristics: sincere character, an unchanged natural disposition, and taking from that which is clear to one while presenting that which is not clear to those who know. If not, then the investigator will perish in those books by rejecting their authors, or by taking something to mean that which it does not.

Understand well.

قاعدة ٣٢ التحذير من كتاب تلبيس إبليس والفتوحات وغيرها

حذر الناصحون من تلبيس ابن الجوزي، وفتوحات الحاتمي بل كل كتبه أو جلها، كابن سبعين، وابن الفارض، وابن أحلا، وابن سودكين، والعفيف التلمساني، والإيكي العجمي، والأسود الأقطع، وأبي إسحاق التجيبي، والششتري، ومواضع من الإحياء للغزالي، جلها في المهلكات منه، والنفخ والتسوية له، والمضنون به على غير أهله، ومعراج السالكين له، والمنقذ، ومواضع من قوت القلوب لأبي طالب المكي، وكتب السهروردي ونحوهم.

فلزم الحذر من مواطن الغلط، لا تَجَنُّبُ الجملة، ومعاداةُ العلم.

ولا يتم ذلك إلا بثلاث: قريحة صادقة، وفطرة سليمة، وأخذ ما بان وجهه، وتسليم ما عداه، وإلا هلك الناظر فيه باعتراض على أهله، أو أخذ الشيء على غير وجه، فافهم.

THE NOTIONS

OF THE SOUL

خواطر النفس

PRINCIPLE 33: NEGATING NOTIONS BY ERECTING EVIDENCE OF THEIR FALSEHOOD CAUSES THEM TO BECOME ENTRENCHED IN THE SOUL. THEY ARE BETTER DISPELLED BY TURNING AWAY FROM THEM.

Seeking to negate concepts by erecting evidence of their falsehood only increases their entrenchment in the soul, because of their antecedence and their conceptualization in the imagination. Thus, what is obvious is that they are only dispelled by leaving them and turning away from them, no matter what they may be or about.

For that reason, Sufyān al-Thawrī said, "Prolong them."

It is said that the Shayṭān is like a dog. If you preoccupy yourself with facing off against him, your skin will get slashed and your robes will be torn. If you take recourse in his Lord, He will divert him from you gently.

One night, during one of my prayers, the following thought came to me: "You are showing off." I opposed that thought from a number of angles. But it did not go away until Allah blessed me to submit to its claim, yet to reject the notion that it occurs in all my works. Consequently, I said, "Confirmation of showing off in this act is a confirmation of sincerity in all the rest. All my works are deficient, and that is the extent of my ability." Thus, it abandoned me immediately.

And all praise is due to Allah.

قاعدة ٣٣ نفي الخواطر بإقامة الحجة على إبطالها يمكنها في النفس ودفعها يكون بالتلهي عنها

قصد نفي الخواطر بإقامة الحجة على إبطالها يزيدها تمكينا في النفس لسبقها وقيام صورتها في الخيال.

فظهر أن دفعها إنما هو بتسليمها والتلهي عنها في أي باب كانت، ومن ثم قال سفيان الثوري: (فزده طولا).

وقال ﷺ: (ليقل الحمد لله الذي رد كيده إلى الوسوسة).

ويقال: (الشيطان كالكلب، إن اشتغلت بمقاومته مزق الإهاب، وقطع الثياب، وإن رجعت إلى ربه صرفه عنك برفق).

وقد جاءني ليلة في بعض الصلوات وقال: إنك مراء، فعارضته بوجوه، فلم يرجع حتى فتح الله بتسليم دعواه وطردها في كل أعمالي بحيث قلت: (إثبات الرياء في هذه إثبات للإخلاص في غيرها، وكل أعمالي معيبة وهذا غاية المقدور، فانصرف عني في ذلك الوقت، ولله الحمد).

PRINCIPLE 34: DISTINGUISHING THE (SOURCE) OF NOTIONS IS FROM THE CONCERNS OF THE PEOPLE OF MURĀQABAH (VIGILANCE) IN ORDER TO REMOVE DISTRACTIONS FROM THE HEART.

Distinguishing the (source) of notions is from the main concerns of the people of *murāqabah* in order to remove distractions from the heart. Thus, it is important for the one who has the most negligible foothold in that (stage) to be concerned with it.

Notions are of four types: 1) Lordly and without an intermediary, 2) egotistical, 3) angelic, and 4) demonic. All only run their course according to His ﷻ power, will, and knowledge.

Lordly notions are neither uprooted nor shaken, just like in the case of egotistical notions. Both can emerge while being directed either at a desired object or at another object. The notion that has to do with special (knowledge of) Divine Oneness is Lordly. That which encourages desires is egotistical. That which corresponds to a legislative principle which is not affected by a legal dispensation or an undisciplined desire is Lordly. Notions other than it are egotistical.

Lordly notions are followed by coolness and expansion, while egotistical notions are anterior to dryness and contraction. Lordly notions are like the dawn that shines forth and only increases clarity. Egotistical notions are like an inanimate pillar. They will either decrease or remain in their state.

As for angelic and demonic notions, they are opposites. Angelic notions only arrive with virtue while demonic notions may also come with good. Thus, there is a degree of ambiguity here. They are distinguished insofar as angelic notions are supported by legal evidences and accompanied by expansions. They are strengthened by remembrance (of God). Their effect is like the light at the time of dawn and they have some permanence. This is different from demonic notions, which are weakened by remembrance (of God) and blinds one from evidences (of

قاعدة ٣٤ تمييز الخواطر من مهمات أهل المراقبة لنفي الصوارف عن القلوب

تمييز الخواطر من مهمات أهل المراقبة لنفي الصوارف عن القلوب فلزم الاهتمام بها لمن له في ذلك أدنى قدم، والخواطر أربعة: رباني بلا واسطة، ونفساني، وملكي، وشيطاني، وكل إنما يجري بقدرته تعالى وإرادته وعلمه.

فالرباني لا متزحزح ولا متزلزل، كالنفساني، ويجريان لمحبوب وغيره، فما كان في التوحيد الخاص فرباني، وفي مجاري الشهوات فنفساني، وما وافق أصلا شرعيا لا تدخله رخصة ولا هوى فرباني وغيره نفساني. ويعقب الرباني برودة وانشراح، والنفساني يبس وانقباض، فالرباني كالفجر الساطع لا يزداد إلا وضوحا، والنفساني كعمود قائم إن لم ينقص بقي على حاله.

وأما الملكي والشيطاني فترددان. ولا يأتي الملكي إلا بخير، والشيطاني قد يأتي به فيشكل، ويفرق بأن الملكي تعضده الأدلة ويصحبه الانشراح، ويقوى بالذّكر، وأثرهُ كغبش الصبح وله بقاء ما، بخلاف الشيطاني، فإنه يضعف بالذكر ويعمى به عن الدليل، وتعقبه حرارة ويصحبه اشتعال وغبار، وضيق، وكزازة في الوقت، وربما تبعه كسل ويأتي من يسار القلب، والملكي عن يمينه، والنفساني من

their falsehood). It is followed by heat and accompanied by feverishness, murkiness, distress, and rigidity in time. It may even be followed by a degree of laziness. It emerges from the left side of the heart while the angelic notion materializes from the right side. The egotistical notion emerges from behind the heart, while in stark contrast the Lordly notion emerges from the front of it.

All, in reality, are divine in origin. However, they are assigned to whatever their association may be. And whatever is free of such connections is attributed to the source. Otherwise, its relationship is judged by its ruling.

Confirmation of this matter is only perfected through spiritual experience. Some have said, "Whoever understands what enters his heart, will recognize the notions that occur in his soul."

And Allah knows best.

خلفه، والرباني مواجه له، والكل رباني عند الحقيقة، ولكن باعتبار النسب فما عرى عنها نسب للأصل، وإلا فنسبته ملاحظة للحكمة.

ثم تحقيق هذا الأمر إنما يتم بالذوق، وقد قالوا: من عقل ما يدخل جوفه عرف ما يهجس في نفسه، والله أعلم.

THE GUIDE AND THE PLEDGE

المرشد والبيعة

PRINCIPLE 35: EVERY SUFI THAT NEGLECTS HIS STATES IN HIS DEALING WITH PEOPLE, ACCORDING TO HOW HE HAS BEEN COMMANDED REGARDING THEM, WILL INEVITABLY FALL INTO ERROR.

Every Sufi that neglects examining his association with people – as he has been commanded to – and turns his face towards the Real without examining His habit with His servants, will inevitably fall into error in his actions, extravagant fantasy in his states, or his statements will be affected by calamities. Thus, he will either perish, be caused to perish, or both will occur to him.

His examination of his connections with people will not be complete for so long as he does not accompany someone who is firmly reputable, a righteous jurist, a knowledgeable disciple, or a sincere friend whom he can use as a mirror for himself. In such a case, if he errs, he will correct him. If he makes a wrongful claim, he will reject it. And if he becomes realized, he will guide him. Such a person will constantly correct his situation. And he will sincerely advise him in all his states, since he will neither suspect him nor neglect him.

Understand well.

قاعدة ٣٥ كل صوفي أهمل أحواله في معاملة الخلق، كما أمر فيها، لابد أن يقع في الغلط

كل صوفي أهمل أحواله من النظر لمعاملة الخلق كما أمر فيها، وصرف وجهه نحو الحق دون نظر لسنته في عباده، فلا بد له من غلط في أعماله، أو شطح في أحواله، أو وقوع طامة في أقواله. فإما هلك أو أهلك، أو كانا معا جاريين عليه.

ولا يتم له ذلك، ما لم يصحب متمكنا، أو فقيها صالحا، أو مريدا عالما، أو صديقا صادقا، يجعله مرآة له، إن غلط رده، وإن ادعى دفعه، وإن تحقق أرشده، فهو ينصفه في حاله، وينصحه في جميع أحواله، إذ لا يتهمه ولا يهمله، فافهم.

PRINCIPLE 36: THE OPENING OF EVERY INDIVIDUAL AND HIS LIGHT CORRESPONDS TO THE OPENING AND LIGHT OF THE ONE HE FOLLOWS.

The opening of every individual and his light will correspond to the opening and light of the one that he follows. Thus, if someone takes knowledge from the one whose condition is from the statements of the scholars alone, his opening and light will be from them.

If he emulates the texts of the Book and the Sunnah, his opening and light will be complete, that is, if he is capable of taking from them both. However, he will lack the light and opening of emulation. That is why the Imams persisted upon [emulation]. Ibn al-Madīnī said, "Ibn Mahdī used to act upon the statement of Mālik. Mālik used to act upon the statement of Sulaymān ibn Yasār. And Sulaymān used to act upon the statement of ʿUmar ibn al-Khaṭṭāb. Thus, the *madhhab* of Mālik was the *madhhab* of ʿUmar."

Al-Junayd said, "Whoever does not listen to Hadith, sit with the jurists, or take his etiquette from the people of good character, those who follow him will be corrupted."

Allah said: "Say: 'This is my path. I called to Allah with insight, I and those who follow me. Blessed is Allah. And I am not of the polytheists.'"[14] And He has also said: "And that this is my straight path. Follow me and do not follow the wayward paths, such that they will separate you from His path. That is what You have been counselled to that perhaps you may be Godfearing."[15]

Understand well.

---

(14) *Yūsuf*, 108.
(15) *al-Anʿām*, 153.

قاعدة ٣٦ فتح كل أحد ونوره على حسب فتح متبوعه ونوره

فتح كل أحد ونوره، على حسب فتح متبوعه ونوره، فمن أخذ علم حاله عن أقوال العلماء مجردة، كان فتحه ونوره منهم، وإن أخذ عن نصوص الكتاب والسنة، ففتحه ونوره تام، إن تأهل لأخذها منهما، ولكن فاته نور الاقتداء وفتحه، ولذلك تحفظ الأئمة عليه كما قال ابن المديني رحمه الله: (كان ابن مهدي يذهب لقول مالك، ومالك يذهب لقول سليمان بن يسار، وسليمان يذهب لقول عمر بن الخطاب، فمذهب مالك إذًا مذهب عمر رضي الله عنهم أجمعين).

وقال الجنيد رحمه الله: (من لم يسمع الحديث، ويجالس الفقهاء، ويأخذ أدبه عن المتأدبين أفسد من اتبعه).

قال تعالى: ﴿قُلْ هَٰذِهِۦ سَبِيلِىٓ أَدْعُوٓا۟ إِلَى ٱللَّهِ عَلَىٰ بَصِيرَةٍ أَنَا۠ وَمَنِ ٱتَّبَعَنِى ۖ وَسُبْحَٰنَ ٱللَّهِ وَمَآ أَنَا۠ مِنَ ٱلْمُشْرِكِينَ ۝١٠٨﴾ الآية، وقال عز من قائل: ﴿وَأَنَّ هَٰذَا صِرَٰطِى مُسْتَقِيمًا فَٱتَّبِعُوهُ ۖ وَلَا تَتَّبِعُوا۟ ٱلسُّبُلَ فَتَفَرَّقَ بِكُمْ عَن سَبِيلِهِۦ ۚ ذَٰلِكُمْ وَصَّىٰكُم بِهِۦ لَعَلَّكُمْ تَتَّقُونَ ۝١٥٣﴾ الآية، فافهم.

PRINCIPLE 37: NO ONE IS FOLLOWED (IN EVERY SINGLE THING) EXCEPT THE SINLESS BECAUSE ERROR HAS BEEN PREVENTED FROM THEM, OR WHOEVER'S EXCELLENCE THEY DECLARE.

Only those who are sinless are followed (in every single matter). This is because error has been prevented from them, or those to whose excellence they have attested. Such is the case since the one recommended by the Just is in fact just.

And he ﷺ has attested that the best of generations is his generation, then those who follow them, and then those who follow them. Thus, their excellence has been confirmed in that very order, followed by those who come after them.

Nevertheless, the Companions dispersed throughout the lands, each of them carrying a certain science, just as Mālik ﷺ said. Consequently, one of them may have a text that abrogates another, while another has the abrogated text. One of them may have an unrestricted text, while the other has a restricted text. Some of them may have universally applicable texts while others have texts that specify their import, as has been evidenced many times.

Thus, it is necessary to take recourse to those after them, that is, those who collected the disseminated texts. And they certified the narrations of them all.

However, though they did accomplish the extraction of jurisprudence from some of them, they did not encompass all of their rulings. As such, it is necessary to take recourse in the third generation because they collected all of that, verified it, and extracted its rulings. Thus, their preservation, correction, and understanding were complete. And all that remained for everyone was to act upon what they had extracted and to accept the principles and foundations that they had established.

And for every science in that generation, there are imams who are famous for their excellence in knowledge and scru-

قاعدة ٣٧ لا متبع إلا المعصوم، لانتفاء الخطأ عنه، أو من شهد له بالفضل

لا متبع إلا المعصوم، لانتفاء الخطأ عنه، أو من شهد له المعصوم بالفضل، لأن وكي العدل عدل.

وقد شهد ﷺ:

(بأن خير القرون قرنه، ثم الذين يلونهم، ثم الذين يلونهم)، فصح فضلهم على الترتيب والاقتداء بهم كذلك، لكن الصحابة تفرقوا في البلاد، ومع كل واحد علم، كما قال مالك رحمه الله:

(فلعل مع أحدهم ما هو ناسخ، ومع الآخر ما هو منسوخ، ومع واحد مطلق، ومع الآخر مقيد، ومع بعضهم عام، وعند الآخر مخصص كما وجد كثيراً).

فلزم الانتقال لمن بعدهم، إذ جمع المتفرق من ذلك، وضبط الرواية فيما هنالك، لكنهم لم يستوعبوه فقهاً، وإن وقع لهم بعض ذلك، فلزم الانتقال للثالث، إذ جمع ذلك وضبطه وتفقه فيه، فتم حفظًا وضبطًا وتفقهًا، فلم يبق لأحد العمل بما استنبطوه، وقبول ما أصلوه واعتمدوه.

ولكل فن في هذا القرن أئمة مشهور فضلهم، علمًا وورعًا كمالك،

pulousness. Among them are Mālik, al-Shāfiʿī, Aḥmad, and Abū Ḥanīfah al-Nuʿmān in jurisprudence; al-Junayd, Maʿrūf, and Bishr in *taṣawwuf*, and al-Muḥāsibī in *taṣawwuf* and theology. For the latter was the first who spoke about affirming the Attributes, as was mentioned by Ibn Athīr.

And Allah knows best.

والشافعي، وأحمد، وأبو حنيفة النعمان للفقه. وكالجنيد، ومعروف، وبشر للتصوف. وكالمحاسبي لذلك وللاعتقادات، إذ هو أول من تكلم في إثبات الصفات، كما ذكره ابن الأثير، والله أعلم.

PRINCIPLE 38: FOR THE CORRECTION OF THE SOUL IT IS NECESSARY TO FOLLOW A SHAYKH IN ORDER TO PREVENT DIVERGENCE AND DEVIATION.

Through a foundation to which one takes recourse in knowledge and action, the correction of the soul is necessary in order to prevent divergence and deviation.

Thus, it is necessary to follow a shaykh whose emulation of the (Prophetic) Sunnah has been confirmed, and who has become established in the area of gnosis, such that he may refer to him in what he receives or seeks, while collecting benefits from others that agree with his foundation. For wisdom is the lost property of the believer. And he is like a bee that is nurtured from every good thing, but only spends the night in its hive. Otherwise, it will not benefit from its honey.

The ascetics (*fuqarā'*) of al-Andalus, from among the later generations, had disputed over the reliance on books to the exclusion of shaykhs. So, they wrote to different lands, and each one responded according to his opening. All the responses revolved around three (principles):

1. It depends on the shaykh. A shaykh of didactic learning (*shaykh al-taʿlīm*) can be replaced by books if a person is intelligent, skilful, and knows the means to knowledge.

A shaykh of spiritual upbringing (*shaykh al-tarbiyah*) can be replaced by accompanying an intelligent, sincere religious person.

A shaykh of spiritual ascension (*shaykh al-tarqiyah*) may be replaced by meeting (the people of God) and deriving blessings.

However, taking them all from a single source is more perfect.

2. It depends on the state of the seeker himself. The unintelligent person must have a shaykh that trains him, while the

قاعدة ٣٨ ضبط النفس بالاقتداء بشيخ لازم لمنع التشعب والتشعث

ضبط النفس بأصل يرجع إليه في العلم والعمل لازم؛ لمنع التشعب والتشعث، فلزم الاقتداء بشيخ، قد تحقق اتباعه للسنة، وتمكنه من المعرفة ليرجع إليه فيما يرد أو يراد، مع التقاط الفوائد الراجعة لأصله من خارج، إذ الحكمة ضالة المؤمن، وهو كالنحلة ترعى من كل طيب ثم لا تبيت في غير جحها، وإلا لم ينتفع بعسلها.

وقد تشاجر فقراء الأندلس من المتأخرين، في الاكتفاء بالكتب عن المشايخ ثم كتبوا للبلاد، فكل أجاب على حسب فتحه. وجملة الأجوبة دائرة على ثلاث:

أولها:

النظر للمشايخ، فشيخ التعليم تكفي عنه الكتب للبيب حاذق الذي يعرف موارد العلم.

وشيخ التربية تكفي عنه الصحبة لدِيّنٍ عاقل ناصح.

وشيخ الترقية يكفي عنه اللقاء والتبرك، وأخذ كل من وجه واحد أتم.

الثاني: النظر لحال الطالب، فالبليد لا بد له من شيخ يربيه، واللبيب

intelligent person may rely on books in his ascension. However, he will not be safe from the deceptions of the soul, even if he arrives at his desired end, because the slave is tested by his esteem for himself.

3. It depends on one's level of struggle. The fear of God does not require a shaykh due to its intelligibility and universal application. However, such worthiness requires a shaykh who can point out which things are more correct and upright. However, a shaykh may be replaced, in the case of an intelligent person, by books, or an avid researcher. However, for ascension, a shaykh is necessary to whom one can take recourse with regard to its illuminations, just as he ﷺ took recourse with Waraqah to present to him what was happening to him due to his knowledge of the matters of prophecy and the early stages of its manifestation, that is, when the Truth came to him suddenly.

This way is close to the first, and the Sunnah is with it.
And Allah knows best.

تكفي الكتب في ترقيه، لكنه لا يسلم من رعونة نفسه، وإن وصل لابتلاء العبد برؤية نفسه.

الثالث: النظر للمجاهدات، فالتقوى لا تحتاج إلى شيخ؛ لبيانها وعمومها، والاستقامة تحتاج إلى شيخ في تمييز الأصلح منها، وقد يكتفي دونه اللبيب بالكتب ومجاهدة الكشف، والترقية لا بد فيها من شيخ يرجع إليه في فتوحها، كرجوعه ﷺ للعرض على ورقة لعلمه بأخبار النبوة ومبادئ ظهورها، حين فاجأه الحق. وهذه الطريقة قريبة من الأولى والسنة معها، والله أعلم.

PRINCIPLE 39: TAKING KNOWLEDGE AND ACTION FROM THE SHAYKHS AND BENEFITTING FROM THEIR ASPIRATION AND STATE.

Taking knowledge and practical teachings from the shaykhs is more complete than taking it from others. "Indeed, it is clear signs in the breasts of those who have been given knowledge."[16] And: "Follow the way of those who constantly turn to Me."[17]

Thus, taking a shaykh is necessary, especially since the Companions took from the Prophet ﷺ, and he took from Jibrīl. He followed his indication in his being a Prophet-Slave and not a Prophet-King. And the Followers (Tābiʿūn) followed the Companions. Each of them had followers who they specially chose, like Ibn Sīrīn, Ibn al-Musayyib, and al-Aʿraj with Abū Hurayrah, Ṭāwūs, Wahb, and Mujāhid with Ibn ʿAbbās, and so on.

As for taking knowledge and action, then its being taken is apparent in what they mentioned and the manner in which they mentioned it.

As for benefitting from the aspiration and the state, Anas indicated it when he said, "We had not yet poured the dirt from our hands to bury him ﷺ when our hearts already changed."

From that report, it is clear that seeing his noble form was beneficial for them in their hearts. The scholars are the inheritors of the Prophets in state and wealth, even if they are not of the same level. And this is the foundation in seeking nearness through the people of Allah in general, because whoever attains a state, those who keep his company can hardly fail to attain it.

That is why we have been commanded to maintain the com-

---

(16)　al-ʿAnkabūt, 49.
(17)　Luqmān, 15.

قاعدة ٣٩ أخذ العلم والعمل عن المشايخ والإفادة من همتهم وحالهم

أخذ العلم والعمل عن المشايخ أتم من أخذه دونهم، ﴿بَلْ هُوَ آيَاتٌ بَيِّنَاتٌ فِي صُدُورِ الَّذِينَ أُوتُوا الْعِلْمَ﴾، ﴿وَاتَّبِعْ سَبِيلَ مَنْ أَنَابَ إِلَيَّ﴾.

فلزمت المشيخة، سيما والصحابة أخذوا عنه ﷺ، وقد أخذ هو عن جبريل،

واتَّبَعَ إشارته في أن يكون: نبيًّا عبدًا لا نبيًّا مَلِكًا، وأخذ التابعون عن الصحابة، فكان لكل أتباع يختصون به، كابن سيرين، وابن المسيب، والأعرج لأبي هريرة، وطاووس، ووهب، ومجاهد لابن عباس إلى غير ذلك.

فأما العلم والعمل، فأخذه جلي فيما ذكروا، وكما ذكروا.

وأما الإفادة بالهمة والحال فقد أشار إليها أنس بقوله:

(ما نفضنا التراب عن أيدينا من دفنه ﷺ حتى أنكرنا قلوبنا)،

فأبان أن رؤية شخصه الكريم، كان نافعًا لهم في قلوبهم، والعلماء ورثة الأنبياء حالًا ومآلًا وإن لم يدانوا المنزلة وهو الأصل في طلب القرب من أهل الله في الجملة؛ إذ من تحقق بحالة لم يخل حاضروه منها،

pany of the righteous and were forbidden from keeping the company of the sinful.
Understand well.

فلذلك أمر بصحبة الصالحين، ونُهِيَ عن صحبة الفاسقين، فافهم.

PRINCIPLE 40: THE CONCLUSION

Our Shaykh, Abū al-ʿAbbās al-Ḥaḍramī said:
"Spiritual education through mechanical means has been lifted. All that remains is benefitting through the aspiration and the spiritual state. As such, it is imperative for you to adhere to the Book and the Sunnah without additions or omissions. And that applies to one's transaction with the Real, his soul, and with the people.

As for one's transaction with the Real, it comprises three things: fulfilling obligations, avoiding prohibited matters, and submitting to the divine decrees.

As for one's transaction with his soul, it also consists of three elements: being objectively upon the truth, abandoning the defence of it, and being weary of its deceptions in what it seeks and what it avoids, what it accepts, and what it rejects, to that which it turns and from that which it flees.

As for one's transaction with people, it also comprises three things: fulfilling their rights, abstaining from what is in their hands, and fleeing from that which will hurt their feelings. The only exception for the latter is the case of an obligatory duty that is unavoidable.

Any disciple who does one of the following is doomed without the possibility of being saved: inclines towards joining the infantry or the means to rectifying the affairs of the general population; busies himself with changing every wrong; concentrates on jihad to the exclusion of other virtues; has frequent times of inaction; desires to encompass all virtues; investigates the hidden matters of his brethren and others, giving the excuse that he is warning; practices the *samāʿ* often; frequents gatherings not for learning or teaching; inclines towards the worldly leaders

قاعدة 40 خاتمة

قال شيخنا أبو العباس الحضرمي: ارتفعت التربية بالإصلاح، ولم يبق إلا الإفادة بالهمة والحال، فعليكم بالكتاب والسنة من غير زيادة ولا نقصان. وذلك جار في معاملة الحق والنفس والخلق.

- فأما معاملة الحق فثلاث: إقامة الفرائض، واجتناب المحرمات، والاستسلام للأحكام.

- وأما معاملة النفس فبثلاث: الإنصاف في الحق، وترك الانتصار لها، والحذر من غوائلها في الجلب والدفع، والرد والقبول، والإقبال والإدبار.

- وأما معاملة الخلق فثلاث: توصيل حقوقهم لهم، والتعفف عما في أيديهم، والفرار مما يغير قلوبهم، إلا في حق واجب لا محيد عنه.

وكل مريد مال لركوب الخيل، أو آثر المصالح العامة، أو اشتغل بتغيير المنكر في العموم، أو توجه للجهاد دون غيره من الفضائل أو معه حالة كونه في فسحة منه، أو أراد استيفاء الفضائل، أو تتبع عورات إخوانه وغيرهم متعللا بالتحذير، أو عمل بالسماع على وجه الدوام، أو أكثر الجمع والاجتماع، لا لتعلم أو تعليم، أو مالَ لأرباب الدنيا بعلة الديانة، أو أخذ بالرقائق والدقائق دون المعاملات، وما

under the guise of religious devotion; is obsessed with the intricacies of the religion and not its practical application and that which rectifies faults; appoints himself to train (the disciples) without being appointed by a shaykh, an imam, or a scholar; follows every preacher and speaker regardless of whether they teach truth or falsehood, without distinguishing his state; disrespects anyone who ascribes himself to Allah, even if he suspects, because of some sign, that he is not truthful; inclines towards dispensations and lenient interpretations; gives precedence to the hidden over the apparent; suffices himself with the apparent over the hidden; brings one of them with that which does not agree with the other; suffices himself with knowledge over action, or with action over state and knowledge, or with the state over them both; anyone who has no foundation to which he returns in his actions, knowledge, state, and practice of the religion, from the accepted foundations in the books of the Imams, such as that of Ibn ʿAṭāʾ Allāh in knowledge of the hidden, especially *al-Tanwīr*, or *al-Madkhal* of Ibn al-Ḥājj in apparent knowledge, or the book of his Shaykh Ibn Abī Jamrah and the realized folk who followed them ﷺ. And whoever adheres to them both, he is a Muslim who will be saved, Allah willing. And protection and success is from Him.

The Messenger of Allah ﷺ was asked about the statement of Allah, 'You are responsible for yourselves,'[18] and he responded, 'If you see greed being obeyed, desires being followed, and every possessor of an opinion being impressed with his own view, then tend to your own

---

(18)   *al-Māʾidah*, 105.

ينبه على العيوب، أو تصدى للتربية من غير تقديم شيخ أو إمام أو عالم، أو اتبع كل ناعق وقائل بحق أو باطل، من غير تفصيل لأحواله، أو استهان بمنتسب إلى الله، وإن ظن عدم صدقه بعلامة، أو مال للرخص والتأويلات، أو قدم الباطن على الظاهر أو اكتفى بالظاهر عن الباطن، أو أتى بأحدهما بما لا يوافق عليه الآخر، أو اكتفى بالعلم عن العمل، أو بالعمل عن الحال والعلم، أو بالحال عنهما، أو لم يكن له أصل يرجع إليه في عمله وعلمه وحاله وديانته من الأصول المسلمة في كتب الأئمة، ككتب ابن عطاء الله في الباطن وخصوصا (التنوير) و(مدخل ابن الحاج) في الظاهر، وكتاب شيخه ابن أبي جمرة، ومن تبعهما من المحققين رضي الله عنهم، فهو هالك لا نجاة له، ومن أخذ بهما فهو ناج مسلم إن شاء الله، والعصمة منه والتوفيق.

وقد سئل رسول الله ﷺ عن قوله تعالى: ﴿عَلَيْكُمْ أَنفُسَكُمْ﴾ الآية. فقال: (إذا رأيت شُحًا مطاعًا، وهوى متبعًا، وإعجاب كل ذي رأي برأيه، فعليك بخويصة نفسك).

وقال عليه الصلاة والسلام في صحف إبراهيم عليه السلام: (وعلى العاقل أن يكون عارفا بزمانه ممسكا للسانه مقبلا على شأنه).

وعلى العاقل أن يكون له أربع ساعات: ساعة يحاسب فيها نفسه، وساعة يناجي فيها ربه، وساعة يفضي فيها إلى إخوانه الذين يبصرونه

121

affairs.'

He ﷺ also said, 'It was written in the Scrolls of Ibrāhīm ﷺ, "It is imperative for the intelligent person to know his time, to restrain his tongue and to focus on his affair.

Thus, it is imperative for the intelligent person to assign for himself four periods of time: a period of time in which he evaluates himself, a period of time in which he pleas intimately upon his Lord, a period of time which he spends with his brethren who will help him with his faults and direct him towards his Lord, and a period of time in which he lets himself enjoy those desires of his that are lawful."' Or as he said it.

May Allah grant us that and assist us towards it. And may He grant us facilitation towards it and cause us to enjoy wellbeing in it. Indeed, we are completely dependent upon the wellbeing He has granted. And He suffices us. And how excellent a guardian. And there is no might nor power except in Allah, the Immensely Great."

May Allah send prayers upon our Master, Mawlānā Muhammad, and upon his Family and Companions and extend them a worthy salutation. And all praise is due to Allah, Lord of all the worlds.

بعيوبه، ويدلونه على ربه، وساعة يخلي فيها بين نفسه وشهوته المباحة، أو كما قال.

رزقنا الله ذلك، وأعاننا عليه، ووفقنا إليه، وصحبنا بالعافية فيه، فإنه لا غنى بنا عن عافيته، وهو حسبنا ونعم الوكيل ولا حول ولا قوة إلا بالله العظيم، وصلى الله على سيدنا ومولانا محمد وعلى آله وصحبه، وسلم تسليما، والحمد لله رب العالمين.

تم بحمد الله